MASTER YOUR MESSAGE LIKE A BOSS BABE

Gizelle Riley teaches smart women how to get the respect, recognition, and money they deserve with personal branding and science-based people skills.

More importantly, she's a Netflix junkie and lives in Kingston, Jamaica with her husband Kevin and sugar dumplin' son Gabe.

This book is perfect for ambitious women who need to get unstuck and stop procrastinating. Your stories hold the key to your success, and Gizelle teaches you how to use them to stand out in a noisy world.

Her unique approach to personal branding shows you how to rewire limiting beliefs, upgrade your people skills, and communicate captivating stories with confidence.

JANETTE BRIN
CARIBBEAN POSH MAGAZINE

I loved how the book flowed. It had me giggling, having some "aha moments". I have a lot of screenshots to refer back to so that I can implement the tips and soak up the wisdom when I need a pick me up or some motivation.

You did an incredible job of breaking down an overwhelming topic into something that makes sense and fun to read.

HEIDI LYNNE KURTER
FORBES SENIOR CONTRIBUTOR

This is a really great book! It reads as if you are speaking to me which I love. Your personal experiences and the advice you give about getting past roadblocks and owning your awesome are important reminders for people like me who sometimes get in their heads.

CHELSEA TENNANT
ISLAND EPICUREAN

Gizelle hits the nail on the head from her introduction. How do you differentiate and add value in a world of fakeness and sameness? She's got me searching for my gems of genius with direction on getting my mind right.

This is the kind of book you're going to want to read slowly and take your time with. I'm even going to recommend that readers have a pen, pencil, sticky notes, a journal, and a long weekend in the hills or by the beach to really dive into the insights you're going to get out of this book.

NATALIE MURRAY
NATALIE MURRAY HEALTH & WELLNESS

Master Your Message Like a Boss Babe is the fast track to creating an authentic, stand out brand and business.

It's not your normal boring how-to build a business in a box kinda book. This is the roadmap that I WISH I had when I first started and it will transform how you think about your message and therefore how you'll be able to stand out as yourself and get paid like a boss.

Gizelle's wisdom, humour, and success combined with her punchy take-aways and straight-up GOLD in messaging know-how make for the most enjoyable read. I devoured the book once I picked it up and I was sad when it ended.

ELISE MAISONNEUVE
ELISE DANIELLE

MASTER YOUR MESSAGE

like a **BOSS BABE**

STEP INTO YOUR POWER
AND ELEVATE YOUR BRAND
ONE STORY AT A TIME

GIZELLE RILEY

Cover and interior design by Gizelle Riley
Photography by Kevin Riley

For more information or speaking engagements, please visit www.gizelleriley.com
or email hello@gizelleriley.com

CONTENTS

MASTER YOUR MESSAGE
like a BOSS BABE

INTRODUCTION

A brand without storytelling reminds me of those cookies I baked when I was 10 years old — tasteless and hard to swallow. Sure, you could smack some jelly on those bad boys but at the end of the day it is what it is — lacking substance.

We live in an era where everyone and their bedazzled chihuahua is pushing a personal brand. Which when you think about it, is pretty fantastic. This contemporary age of media has given us the power to showcase our awesomeness and build empires from our little slice of internet heaven.

Here's the problem, it's made the digital world a playground for cookie-cutter personas and downright fake crap.

If you're on a mission to build a magnetic brand, you have to be strategic *and* authentic.

As much as you adore the content your favourite influencer posts about their fabulous life in Bali running a 6-figure business, it kind of gets less thrilling after a while. The reason is because everyone seems to share the same kind of stories. You see all the magic and none of the mess.

Think about someone you admire online, it doesn't have to be a celebrity. Even if they don't show up on your feed, you'll do a quick search for them every now and then. It's still fresh in your mind that time they shared a video featuring their bambino causing a naptime tantrum. Looking visibly pooped, the object of your admiration admitted that they used to judge other mothers who couldn't control their children in similar situations. Oh, how things have changed.

As a new member of Club Mommy, that 1-minute story put things into perspective. It gave you the grace to not live up to society's standard of what a perfect mother looks like. That peek into a very personal moment let you know that under all the poopy diapers and sleepless nights, you weren't alone.

It's the mess that builds real connections. Now, I'm not saying to share that time you let go a bomber in public and blamed your husband for the foul stench to which he was mercilessly vilified. What I'm saying is that if you're on a mission to build a magnetic brand, you have to be strategic *and* authentic. Or in other words, show the magic *and* the mess.

THOU SHALT GET OFF THY BUTT

I believe that we all have the capacity to be a success. The dreams we have are there for a reason. There's a powerhouse leader inside of us just begging to come out. But we've drowned her voice out with doubt. We miss out on our calling due to a lack of clarity and action.

When I hit age 30, I entered into what I guess you could call a post-quarter life crisis. I got really tired of seeing other people get promotions I knew I was best suited for. I was an anxious mess over the fact that after the meteoric rise and fall of my first business at age 21, I was too scared to pursue another venture. I was also tired of being super cheap. I would rather scour the bowels of Google than invest in myself and pay for online courses.

There were many nights I spent crying on my bathroom floor asking God for a change. Why weren't my vision boards working? I was a good person. Didn't I deserve to get exactly what I wanted out of life? One night I finally got an answer. He told me to get off my butt, stop wasting time in victim-mode and just do something. Anything. The clock was ticking. I didn't want to spend another 30 years like this. So I dragged myself off the floor and started taking action.

Some of the phenomenal results since that night include getting promotions, tripling my income, creating a podcast that educates and inspires thousands of women across the globe, and finally living within my purpose of supporting ambitious women through my personal branding and success coaching practice. This happened all within two years.

The stories we tell ourselves are equally as important as the ones we tell the world.

I smile when I look back at that skinny girl wearing her mother's one-size-too-big work clothes, optimistically walking downtown in the blazing sun with job applications in hand. I know she'd be proud of her future self and excited for what comes next.

How did everything turn around? Did I wave a wand from Hogwarts and say abracadabra on my life? No. I started to take aligned action into finding my *story*. I needed to know what makes me tick. What gave me energy. I needed to build my confidence. I went on a journey of deconstruction to build a better version of myself, someone who was prepared to receive the things she prayed for.

BOSS BABE (noun): a powerhouse woman who attracts success by being her amazing self.

Once I jumped down the rabbit hole of my soul, I was able to shape myself into a magnetic brand — one that continues to attract the right people and opportunities into my personal and professional life.

STORIES ARE POWERFUL MOTIVATORS

Your unique experiences can change someone's perspective, give them a jolt to finally take action, or provide the answer to a nagging question they had in an instant.

I remember laying on my couch watching a Lisa Nichols webinar one summer afternoon in what felt like 100 degree heat. She shared her story of rising from rock bottom as a single mother on government assistance, to investing in her personal development by attending seminars, and eventually impacting people worldwide as a motivational speaker. Did I mention she became a multi-millionaire? That too.

This wasn't the first time I heard her story but something clicked for me at that moment. I remember looking to my right at the old air conditioning unit and feeling ticked off that I had to resist the urge to turn it on to save some coins. I also kept thinking about my own mother, and feeling overwhelming gratitude for the sacrifices she made.

There were a bunch of other emotions floating around inside of me, but I mostly remember feeling inspired. Heck, if she did it with less then what's stopping me? Nothing, that's what. It pushed me to dust off my laptop and recommit to finish writing this book. Now if that isn't inspired action, I don't know what is.

YOU ARE A MULTI-SENSORY EXPERIENCE

Most of the time, we're conditioned to dance on that fine line of acceptance. We don't want to be polarizing and share too much of who we are for fear of not being liked. But guess what, we like people a whole lot more when we know where they stand.

It's like that coworker Janet who always tries to be neutral. You may like her for a quick lunchroom laugh, but you don't respect her. She consumes office gossip from everyone, but when it comes to having an opinion in public, she'll play the "I see both sides" card.

You can't trust someone you don't know, someone who sits on the fence. Any monkey can see both sides of something, but that doesn't stop them from choosing to stuff their face with a banana over an apple.

Mastering your message means taking 360° ownership of how you communicate.

55% of communication is non-verbal?[1] This goes to show that storytelling extends *way* beyond what you're saying or posting on social media. Every day you're telling the story of your character, which is the foundation of your influence.

---

[1] Imram Tariq (2019) *4 Ways to Close Sales with Non-Verbal Communication:* Entrepreneur

When you master something, you're in control. So when you master your message, it means that you're constantly evaluating and managing the stories you're sending out to the world, even the non-verbal ones.

GREAT STORIES DON'T REQUIRE CREDENTIALS

Gone are the days where reciting your résumé was enough to drive business to your brand.

Scratch that. Those days never existed.

People may respect your education but they *connect* with your story. Have you ever been moved by someone's story and said to yourself, "Wow, that was really inspiring. I wonder if they have credentials for that experience?"

I'm 99.99% sure you haven't.

How you share yourself tells people more of who you are than any piece of paper can. People want to work with someone who gets them. Someone who can identify with where they're at in their journey. How you tell your story shows them you have the tools to get them to a higher level. Basically, you represent the growth that can happen for them.

Wanting to be seen as an expert doesn't mean removing your personality from the equation.

You may wonder if great stories live inside you. I'm here to tell you that they're there. Trust me. You have a lifetime worth of chaotic, heart wrenching, and inspiring moments to make a binge-worthy Netflix series. There are gems of genius inside of you. You simply need to bring them to the surface.

STRATEGIC STORYTELLING

Imagine that you're a world-class archer. You've spent years training, finally made it to the Olympics, but when it came time to let-er-rip there was no target. Sounds crazy right? It's the same as having a vague idea of your *signature story*.

Your signature story is the anchor of your brand; a point of reference that guides your strategic storytelling. Without one, you may find yourself racking your brain for content and sharing random posts on social media that make no sense. It's like talking about your cat Buttons when you have a catering company. Unless Buttons loves your herb-roasted chicken that's going on sale, she has no place on your feed.

When I started out in my early days as a blogger, I nearly killed myself with all the random content I churned out week after week. One moment I was writing a post about my favourite books, then another would be about the latest trends in digital marketing, followed by an ebook on herbal remedies for colds, and God knows what else. I was making a lot of noise and no one was listening.

Operating within a niche would have provided direction, but at the time I felt being exclusive would limit my opportunities. Take it from me, if you try to cater to everyone, you'll work with no one. If you do happen to get a client, they're not likely going to be your cup of tea because you weren't specific from the beginning on who *you* want to work with.

Listen, you don't need to have a fast-paced hustle mentality when it comes to content creation. There will always be people doing similar work to yours, teaching similar things, and selling similar products. What makes you stand out and gets people fired up to work with you is the person behind the content.

Do any of these sound familiar?

You're stuck in analysis paralysis. You're a multi-talented and multi-skilled woman so it's been hard selecting what gift you want to share with the world — your genius.

You've been scouring Google and YouTube for answers. But all those free webinars and dated blog posts have left you drained and even more confused about your brand identity.

Your stories don't seem to resonate with your audience. You've been hustling like crazy and have been throwing all your time and money into advertising, social media, and blog posts with little results.

You haven't identified your people. You want to find your niche, but either don't know how to find your people or are too scared to get granular because you think doing that will limit your opportunities for growth and monetization.

You're losing your motivation. You worry that there are just too many experts online already. You find yourself wondering how many services like yours does the world really need.

Whether you're training for the Olympics or building a business, the only way to hit targets is to first know where you're aiming. Discovering your signature story provides the clarity and confidence needed to kiss these nagging issues goodbye.

BECOME THE ARCHITECT OF YOUR SUCCESS

If your company went under tomorrow, would you freak out? There's a certain level of freedom that comes with being recognized as an expert or industry leader. You become a magnet for opportunities. You wouldn't sweat a closure notice because you already have people on the backend sending emails requesting your services.

Being the architect of your success starts with taking ownership of yourself as a brand. I promise that once you're finished reading this work-of-heart that every move you make moving forward will be geared toward creating equity. This is true whether you're an employee *or* entrepreneur.

An example of equity is Marie Forleo getting paid thousands of dollars for a 15-minute presentation and a relatively unknown college professor getting paid in gratitude for the same thing. There is equity in your expertise and experience, but only if people know about it.

Sister, you're a soul-centred ambitious woman who wants to make lives better with her gifts.

Heck, you want to make money too. Deep down, you know that:

- You're ready to get clarity on your purpose and the confidence that goes with it.

- You're called to be a magnetic leader that inspires your team and colleagues.

- You have a burning desire to make a positive impact and attract your dream clients.

- You're ready to upgrade your people skills and become a persuasive communicator.

- You're ready to be seen as a respected industry expert by the media.

- You're ready to network and connect with people in a way that leaves you feeling energized and motivated.

Here's something you should know about me: I hate fluff. I wrote this book with you in mind, but also myself. It had to be something I would want to read and rave about. Thankfully those late nights and working lunches weren't in vain because I can confidently say that you'll take away some major nuggets of wisdom.

Think of *Master Your Message Like A Boss Babe* as a practical guide for elevating your personal brand. It will teach you actionable psychology-backed storytelling strategies and people skills to increase your impact and influence.

Here's something it *doesn't* do: provide surface level advice. You're going to work on some deep stuff that steps outside the box of traditional personal branding approaches. You won't find information on how to dress or what colours to use for your website. While those are important, this book focuses on upgrading your mindset and interpersonal communication skills so that there's no question in anyone's mind that you're the go-to expert who's worth the big bucks.

There's more inside than you're sharing. After years of playing small, you're finally ready to bulldoze through your goals, look fear in the face, and give it a big "screw you". Take this book as a sign that you're on the right track.

CHAPTER ONE

SHE'S THE [BADASS EXPERTISE] LADY

Your reputation is power.

You may think it's your expertise, but the reality is that other people can do what you do. Sometimes even better.

As humans, we build narratives about people, our environment, and ourselves. We need to give meaning to everything so that we can navigate this big, scary, beautiful world.

Just because Superman could fly around the globe, throw a cement mixer, and warm coffee with his heat vision, doesn't mean that his buddies from Krypton couldn't do the same thing. The real power was his reputation. He was Earth's saviour from intergalactic baddies.

Why do you think Lex Luthor tried to expose his identity? Because Clark Kent was ordinary. Or as ordinary as someone with powers can be. If the people of Metropolis found out, the image they have in their minds would be skewed. Ordinary people are subject to laws. So even though he saved the city, you may start to wonder if this human-looking alien has a green card.

We want to be inspired. But we also want to put people in categories. Can you imagine the scandal if you found out that Princess Diana didn't actually give a crap about the less fortunate? It would rock your reality. She was *The People's Princess*. By the way, this is why smear campaigns for celebrities are systematic. If you can't beat the (wo)man, you beat the brand.

CONTROL THE NARRATIVE

Let's say that you're really good at social media marketing. It's your passion. You know you're good because you've done freelance work for friends and family who get a major return on their investment. You're constantly taking courses to improve your skills. You'd love to transition to the marketing department of your company. But here's the thing, you work in accounting. No one knows about your badass expertise. All they know is that you're responsible for getting their salaries into their accounts on time each month.

Your story isn't just what you tell people, it's what they believe.

One day, you see a suave looking lady in skinny jeans and stilettos enter your office. She's the new social media consultant. You didn't even know that the position was available. Your CEO constantly raves about her, which leaves you very confused. Not to be a hater, but you know what she's doing is basic stuff and that you could do way better.

Even if you voice that you've got the goods, because you haven't cultivated a reputation around it, no one's going to listen or take you seriously. All they want from you is to stop making noise and crunch numbers.

Is it fair? Maybe. After all, she put in the work to build her reputation which is why the higher-ups brought her in as a consultant. It would have been nice if your CEO and colleagues took you seriously, but you really can't blame them. The fact that they've painted a picture of what you represent in their mind is on you.

CLAIM YOUR SUPERPOWER

Your personal brand can be your downfall or competitive edge. Amazon CEO Jeff Bezos is widely quoted as saying that "your brand is what people say about you when you're not in the room". Here's what you want them to say:

"I know her. She's the [badass expertise] lady"

When we think of that hippie friend who's always trying a new craze because they heard that eating sea sand was great for their health, or that horrid boss who makes you work overtime by breathing down your neck minutes before you're about to cut loose, you've branded them.

You yourself have been branded by the string of stories on Google. Did you know that 93% of employers will search for a candidate's social media profile during the interview?[2] Business leaders aren't exempt as 44% of a company's market value is attributable to the CEO's reputation.[3] Take a minute to search for your

---

[2] Ashley Stahl (2018) *Why Personal Branding is key to Career Success*: Forbes

[3] Ryan Erskine (2017) *Does Your CEO Have A Personal Brand? If not, it could be affecting your bottom line*: Forbes

name, check out what it has to say and take notes. Do you like what you see? Are you even there?

Strategic storytelling is perfect for search engine optimization (SEO) because it's a means of creating evergreen keyword-rich content. Here are some easy hacks to keep your SEO game strong:

- **Make your LinkedIn profile public.** LinkedIn pushes you up the ranking for first and last name searches. If it ain't on Google what's the point, right?

- **Write guest blog posts for high-traffic websites.** Outside of SEO, sharing your expertise on other websites exposes your brand to new audiences and positions you as a thought-leader.

- **Submit your website to Google Webmaster.** Yes, you need a website if you're serious about building a profitable personal brand. Submitting your domain makes search engine crawlers index your content faster under multiple keywords, giving your ranking a boost.

- **Optimize content with keyword phrases.**
  Think about what people are searching for,
  and include those words and phrases in
  your content. Do this for the file names of
  images and videos too.

We live our lives mostly not giving much thought
to our reputation. Though it may not matter if you
seem ditzy to your best friend, that may not be the
impression you want to give to potential clients.
That being said, you don't have to be straight-
laced and wear suits like everyone else. That's a
recipe for a boring-ass brand.

Maybe your gift is to make people laugh like JP
Sears with his *Ultra Spiritual* videos. Or you're a
Bawse like Lilly Singh, empowering humans to
become super-confident. Whatever your
superpower, the only way you can take ownership
of it is by understanding what motivates you on a
psychological and spiritual level. Yup, it's that
deep.

YOU'RE NOT FOR EVERYONE

...and that's a good thing. Have you ever had to
deal with a coworker whose work ethic was way

different than yours? You want to start executing on the big project to meet the deadline, when all they want to do is take long lunches and complain about why your boss gave it to you in the first place. If you knew how they were beforehand, you would have declined partnering with them.

It's the same if you're an entrepreneur. When I hosted my first *Brand Storytelling for Boss Babes* workshop, I was extremely selective about who I wanted to participate. I wanted positive, mission-driven women who were ready to dominate their digital brand.

A few days before the event, I got a call from what sounded like a very mature lady asking about the lesson plan. Once I told her, she kept asking why I decided on that curriculum and suggested that it would be better if I taught people how to use social media. Ummm, ok. This was a signal to end the conversation. She was a Negative Nancy. Plus, this event was for women who already knew how to use social media. Instead of telling her to stop wasting my time and get the fudge off my phone, I politely told her that this workshop wouldn't be for her. I could hear the shock in her voice as her gasp pierced my ears. The fact is, I didn't want to work with someone I knew wouldn't make use of my knowledge. I wasn't for her and she *definitely* wasn't for me.

When you know who you are and what you offer, you can avoid potential disastrous affiliations. You can also magnetize opportunities and relationships that are aligned with your authentic self.

HAVE YOU BEEN HOLDING YOURSELF BACK?

You want to increase your impact, influence *and* income. But to do that, *you have to raise the value of your work*. You can have degrees, experience, and connections up the wazoo, but if you haven't confidently positioned yourself as an expert, you won't have the street cred to set your price.

People fork over thousands of dollars to work with consultants if they believe that they can deliver results. The ones interested in working with you want a sense of security that they're not wasting their time and money. This is why getting your mind right is critical to how you present yourself to the world. More often than not, people are going to believe what you tell them. However, if you say one thing and uncertainty drips from your pores, you've already lost.

Keep everything in perspective. Realistically, you may not be the best pastry maker in the world. But if you know deep down that your apple pies create a transcendent experience, the world ought to know it. Ask yourself these questions whenever you start to feel a twinge of doubt:

1. Do people need my work?
2. Will the world be a better place having it?

If the answers are NO, you need to reevaluate which expertise you want to lead with. But if the answers are YES, ask yourself if you're a selfish prick. Since you're reading this book, that answer's going to be NO, which means that it's time to stop hiding and take action.

Stop telling yourself that it could be better and start owning your badass expertise.

Personal branding is just that – personal. One of the main reasons why so many flop is because people's internal narrative doesn't match the external one. Since we got that covered, see if you've been making these other common mistakes:

Inconsistency: There's no focused message. You're all over the place. One minute you're presenting yourself as a health guru and the next you're a social media maven. The types of images, language used, and colours change as often as you change your clothes. Being multi-passionate is great but you have to have a strategy to let it stay under one umbrella. When it comes to your target audience, if you confuse them, you lose them.

Lack of knowledge: Do you actually know what you're talking about? No one will ever know everything about their field of expertise. But if you pull a Hail Mary and decide to become a relationship expert when the last good one you had was when Obama was in office, you may not be the right person for the job.

Lack of communication skills: Are you engaging with your tribe on and offline? How does your brand align with your verbal and body language? Having a lack of communication skills can also mean that you aren't able to clearly and confidently put your point across in conversations.

Being unrealistic: Building a powerhouse brand takes time. Looking at Gary Vaynershuck's empire and trying to do-all-the-things can leave you burned out. Remember, he built his brand over the course of several years. Unless you have the manpower and the marketing budget to accommodate an immense and constant stream of content, you ought to be easy on yourself with those goals.

Dishonest or bad behaviour: This should be obvious. Besides being unethical, it's best to remember that nothing is ever hidden forever. Word gets around. People follow and work with who they trust. Once that credibility is shot, you can kiss future opportunities goodbye. Don't claim to be some hot-shot dentist when the majority of past clients hate your services, or if you have fudged up teeth. Don't claim to be a faith-based entrepreneur when you're hitting the clubs in sequined shorts each weekend. Bad behaviour can translate online. Even retaliating in an undignified way to negative comments or internet trolls is not a good look.

DON'T WALK AROUND WITH A SUCKY BRAND

People with magnetic brands are crystal clear about who they are. Going deep on discovering your stories will provide the confidence and clarity to make that your reality. But since people need to be captivated with your presence before they connect with you, take some time to appraise and upgrade your existing brand before moving onto the next section.

PHASE 1: CREATE A VISION OF SUCCESS

Do you want people to see you as a master photographer? Do you dream of being invited to Australia to speak at a women's leadership conference? What does that version of you look like?

Write down how you see your brand right now, then compare it with a description of how you want it to be. Think along the lines of your personality, interests, experience and credentials. Do they match up? Make note of inconsistencies.

You can identify people whose personal brand resonates with you. Note the qualities you admire most and use them as benchmarks to guide designing your powerhouse presence.

PHASE 2: SEE THE BIG PICTURE

Take screenshots of the visual pieces of your brand, like your website homepage, logo, profile pictures, social media and blog post images, PDF resources, etc. Copy and paste your messages, this includes your tagline, about page biography, and recent social media and blog posts.

Once you're done, shrink to fit everything within one document like a map. The objective is to see how everything looks as a whole to help you determine what adds or subtracts from your brand. Setting up a private Pinterest board is another option for laying out these elements.

PHASE 3: REVIEW YOUR "SEARCHABILITY"

Do a first and last name search online and see what comes up. This includes making note of where you rank in the results, what images appear, and the accessibility of your social media pages. Extend your search to include your geographic location.

After jotting down your findings, search for your expertise and see what your competitors are doing. Identify common keywords associated with your industry. You can use these to support your SEO and content creation in the future.

PHASE 4: GET UP CLOSE AND PERSONAL

How does the world see you? Ask friends, family, and people you work with to describe you in five words. Since first impressions count, even ask a few strangers. Also, get feedback on your messages and visual identity based on the document you created earlier.

One of the most important questions you can ask is: *What do you think I do?* If people are unable to figure out your expertise off the bat, that's a sign you need to make some tweaks to your messaging.

PHASE 5: REVIEW, DECLUTTER, UPGRADE

Review the information gathered along each step. Does your brand align with your vision? Make changes and do damage control where necessary. This includes deleting photos, changing account names, email addresses, and updating biographies.

This is the perfect time to start eliminating anything you're doing that doesn't support your vision. If you see yourself as a leader, stop asking for permission to get things done.

CHAPTER TWO

CLEAR OUT THE CLUTTER

FACT: Women tend to not know their worth. Did you know that women are 16% less likely to apply for a job even if they meet every requirement?[4] Here's the interesting part, studies show that they have a better shot of getting hired over their male counterparts. No one knows the origin for this *confidence gap*, but what we do know is that women are far more capable than they give themselves credit for.

FACT: Your value doesn't come from industry qualifications. Sure, these go a long way in positioning yourself as an expert. But guess what, no one puts you on a pedestal. You have to declare that you've got the goods on your own and consistently tell the world about it. Do you think Tiffany Haddish went to *Comedian University* to learn how to make people laugh? No.

---

[4] Maria Ignatova. *LinkedIn Talent Solutions* (2019) Gender Insights Report: *How women find jobs differently*

FACT: You're the reason why you're not who (and where) you want to be. I don't need empirical evidence to back this up. You're a smart person, you know this.

You can create a sound growth strategy, have high power connections, and be a genius at what you do, but if you lack confidence, fear will give you every excuse in the book why you're not achieving your goals. What helps you build confidence? Clarity.

We all suffer from *clarity roadblocks*. But since we never gave them names, it was hard to recognize when they sprung up to kick them to the curve. These pesky troublemakers prevent us from standing in our power and finding our story.

LIMITING THOUGHTS

We all know what limiting thoughts are. It's those little monsters that whisper in our ears, saying things like:

- You're not enough.

- Who do you think you are to want that?

- You don't deserve it.

- You're not as good as they are.

- You're not ready yet.

- Maybe people will like a slimmer version.

- You can't be yourself because people won't like you.

- It's too late to pursue your dreams.

- People don't value what you have to offer.

Just typing these gets me riled up. I could go on, but you get the picture. These kinds of thoughts can be crippling. I've found that the best way to counteract the crap that comes to our minds is to affirm what's real.

When I set out to host my first workshop I was extremely nervous. I had several other presentations under my belt working in corporate, but this was different. This was *my* voice. I battled with so many questions of worthiness.

Limiting Thought #1: Maybe I shouldn't do the workshop because I only have a small group of followers.

Limiting Thought #2: People will laugh at me.

Limiting Thought #3: I'm 6 months pregnant. Maybe I should put it off till I look less fluffy in pictures.

Limiting Thought #4: I really can't afford it. Suppose no one comes and I end up being out of pocket.

Thanks to prayer, support from loved ones, and just being tired of getting in my own way, I forged ahead and counteracted those lies with what was true.

Growth Thought #1: It doesn't matter if you have a small group of followers. Everyone starts at zero. There are people out there who need what you have to offer. Get over your shit. You're doing this for them and not for you.

Growth Thought #2: People have their own lives and the naysayers are not that invested to laugh at you. Even if they are, screw 'em. Your people need you.

Growth Thought #3: If Cardi B can girate on stage pregnant, you can host a workshop. Need clothes that fit? Buy 'em. Embrace the beautiful fluff, you're growing a human. Besides, maybe you'll inspire other pregnant women to put themselves out there.

Growth Thought # 4: We afford what we want. Did you really need to go to that restaurant for the shrimp fettuccine? No. Use your marketing skills to fill those seats.

The workshop was fan-tabulous. Even better than I expected. Sure, the seats were filled and I made a profit, but it was more than just an occasion to share my expertise. It was an experience filled with inspiration, tears, laughter, and sisterhood. Can you imagine if I made those limiting thoughts stop me? I wouldn't have met those great women and they would have had to spend years figuring out how to accelerate their brand.

The best way to counteract the crap that comes to our minds is to affirm what's real.

Along with affirming what's real, you need to constantly engage in activities that cultivate a *success mindset*. Having one keeps you on track with your goals. Ever went to a leadership seminar and left feeling like you could change the world? We all have. We tell ourselves that we're going to stop doubting our greatness, get serious about our career, and basically become the person we always dreamed of being.

Two days later you hit the snooze button on your alarm because you need a few extra Zzzs. You held your tongue when your co-worker made a snide remark at your expense. You even decided to put off doing that online course because you felt it was a bit out of your budget. You start to fall into the same trap of stagnation.

Habits are funny things, and can be hard to break. Here's my advice, instead of trying to break them, start including new ones each day that contribute to your growth. When you get that feeling of inspiration coupled with a splash of discipline on a daily basis your subconscious will take notice and your actions will start to change. Eventually, those nagging habits that limit your potential will evaporate.

Here are some activities you can include in your routine:

- Listen to a podcast in your car on the way to work

- Record personal affirmations on your phone and listen to it while you're on your lunch break and/or right before you go to sleep

- Go on YouTube and watch motivational and educational videos of people you admire

LIMITING BEHAVIOUR

Your thoughts influence your behaviour and vice versa. You can tell yourself that you're amazing but if your actions say otherwise your subconscious is going to believe the latter. If this is a major roadblock, you likely suffer from the dreaded *self-sabotage*.

Do any of these ring a bell?

- Starting a project then not completing it
- Having great ideas that only live your journal
- Not charging what you feel your service is worth
- Over delivering to your clients and feeling burned out
- Not sharing personal parts of yourself because you worry that you won't be liked

The solution to fighting limiting behaviour is to get uncomfortable. This goes for your personal and professional life. As much as you try to compartmentalize, nothing is mutually exclusive. It's why you go home and complain to your partner about work, and tell Sheila about how you wish Jason would wash the dishes after dinner.

If you have a tendency of undercharging for your services when you know that you're providing transformational value, do the uncomfortable thing and charge what it's worth. Though this can depend on your business model, having an offering that's seen as cheap will either repel premium clients or reduce sales overall. No one wants to be associated with cheap. It's why people will spend a month's salary to purchase an iPhone.

The medicine for combating limiting behaviour is to do uncomfortable things.

If your manager made a passive aggressive comment, don't disregard it. Do the uncomfortable thing and calmly ask what they meant by what they said in the moment. Honestly, if they said that you've done so well for someone with your education level, you know what they meant. Take your power back and don't let them off the hook. Here's how you can throw their question back at them:

"When you said I've done well for my education level, are you saying that you didn't expect me to be intelligent because I didn't go to college?"

Sounds assertive, right? Good. You started off by repeating their actual words, and ended the question with an extreme perspective. One part allows them to reflect on their words, and the other puts them on guard for a potential report to human resources. By probing about their intention you mess up their equilibrium. These kinds of people usually don't expect someone to question them so when they are they tend to retreat. Do this enough, they'll avoid bothering you.

But what if they're brazen enough to own up to what they were saying? Here's how you respond:

"I never thought of you as the kind of person who would attack someone. Let me apologize if I gave you the impression that we have anything more

than a strictly professional relationship. Moving forward, I'd like to keep it that way."

As you can see, you started out by addressing their character. No one likes being seen other than a paragon of virtue, even bullies. Next, you apologize if your behaviour gave them a false impression that saying those kinds of things are fine (even if you never felt like you did it's best to cover your bases). You round out your response out by letting them know in a diplomatic way that you want nothing more to do with them.

As for more personal matters, limiting behaviour can even be disguised as politeness. If your toxic relative gives you a Christmas present (that you don't even like) don't say you love it. Say thank you and keep it moving.

Doing the uncomfortable thing will seem scary at first, but it's a practice that has to be done so that you can value *yourself* and build your confidence.

JANE OF ALL TRADES

I get it. You rock. You're good at so many things, might as well do 'em. Besides, maybe if you offer a range of services that tickle your interests and utilizes your multitude of talents you can get more dough in your bank account.

Sorry friend, but it doesn't exactly work that way.

If you do your research you'll find that super successful people often started out work on one offering at a time. As their income grew, they were able to expand their interests in a bigger way.

I remember when I started my business a couple of years ago I did everything. Need me to build a website? Sure. Need copywriting? Absolutely. Want me to clean up your inbox? No problemo.

My brand was all over the place. I was capable and could get money from it so why not, right? The problem was that I was burned out and angry. I was not operating within my zone of genius. On top of that, being all over the place limited my opportunities to get clients I actually wanted to work with.

It wasn't until I cut all the crap out. I finished up jobs with clients and took a real zen moment to breathe and search for what made me happy. It seemed crazy at the time because I was turning down some mucho dinero. But that was what I needed to get focused.

SECOND OPINIONS

Ah yes, the final roadblock: *second opinions.*

This one is a doozy. You have to walk a fine line between what feedback is valuable and what needs to be left behind. Keep in mind that even the best intended piece of advice can slow down your progress because the people giving it may be influenced by their own roadblocks.

Imagine if Serena Williams stopped playing tennis because a family member said her swerve was too aggressive. Or if Rihanna didn't pursue an international music career because a friend back home told her that it was unlikely for a Caribbean artist to hit it big.

You have to be selective. Not everyone is equipped to guide you. Don't ask Sharon if she thinks speaking at an event is a good career move if she's worked at the same job and position for the past decade.

Too many dreams never see the light of day because we are too afraid of what the wrong people would think, even if we see them as gatekeepers. I once interviewed a really compelling storyteller named Jackie. She told me that in the early days of her career as a professional writer, she sent a pitch that was mercilessly shut down. It was brutal, they basically annihilated her writing. Sure, it hurt for a quick second, but she didn't take it personally. She got a writing coach to help improve her craft, re-pitched and got published in the same magazine that turned her down. Now she writes for major global publications like Forbes, Fast Company and Entrepreneur. She could have let the feedback stop her. If she did, the world wouldn't have had the chance to be inspired by her work. Thank God she didn't listen.

Before seeking advice, appraise the source. If you need a reminder that you're a slice of awesome and you know your Grandma Mary is a constant spring of encouragement then go for it. Sometimes we need a pep up. But for advice on advancing your career, be more strategic. You don't want the wrong thing to get into your head to fester. The best way to combat the roadblock of second opinions is by being decisive. Ask yourself the following questions before absorbing opinions:

- Is this the best person to be giving me advice?

- Is their advice valuable to my development?

- Does it make me feel uncomfortable?

- Is the advice in alignment with my goals?

- What does my gut say about my next move?

BREAK THE CYCLE

What are the underlying beliefs and behaviour that keep you from moving forward? Review your year to identify counterproductive patterns. Make note of the reasons why you haven't accomplished some of your original goals. You may feel some resistance, and that's fine. You have to face the monsters before you slay them. Since clarity roadblocks take root in our psyche over time, take it a step further and consider the earliest instances in your life when those patterns started taking root.

Doing this exercise will show you which roadblocks to work on. Think of it like going to the doctor's office. Once you've found what's making you sick, go over what you learned about each roadblock and take the prescribed medicine. This is your time to replace the lies that have been holding you back with what's true.

CHAPTER THREE

TRAIN YOUR BRAIN TO FOCUS

If you have a heart condition, would you go to a general practitioner or a cardiologist?

You would go to the cardiologist because you want a specialist. You even pay them more than you would a regular doctor because you know that they have the expertise to work on your ticker.

This is how you want to stand out in people's minds. But it's hard being a multi-talented woman. Your head is chock full of creative ideas. No wonder it's difficult to focus on just one project at a time, let alone decide how you want to present your personal brand to the world.

Don't beat yourself up. It's in our DNA. We're so used to doing everything. We give so much of ourselves to our family, our jobs, and our children, that when the time comes to get down and do our own thing we go haywire. Doing something for ourselves seems like a foreign concept.

Think of your day in terms of blocks of time. Let's say you only have five blocks per day. Now imagine yourself at your computer ready to work. You want to create a lead magnet. You've already done the research and have the copy in hand. All that's left to do is to put it together. Let's say that it will take five blocks to complete. That's one whole day. Let's label the task as the letter A with each different task having a different letter.

You start off strong on getting it done, there goes a block. Then you see a webinar you think could help with sales calls, there goes another block. After that, you get inspired to do some research on the person who presented the webinar - another block used.

Finally, you go back to working on your lead magnet. But then you get a call that you simply have to take - another block out the window.

Oops. You've spent all your blocks of time and have been derailed from your original objective.

Take a look. Didn't accomplish much did you? And that was just a simple example. You know way more things grab your attention and take up your time throughout the day.

A	B	C	A	D

Weeks, maybe even months roll by and that lead magnet never sees the light of day. Eventually, negative self-talk rears its ugly head and you wonder if you were cut out to create this thing in the first place.

It's not your fault. No one taught you how to train your brain to focus; you're used to doing a million other things. It may not be your fault, but it is your responsibility to fix it.

STOP OVERESTIMATING WHAT YOU CAN GET DONE

Great brands, personal or otherwise, aren't built overnight. There's no get-rich-quick scheme for building a profitable brand. Remember, Oprah wasn't always *Oprah*. Don't get me wrong, you can position yourself as an expert right now. But what's the point of being branded and broke?

You CAN do everything your heart desires... just not at the same time.

There are levels to success, but the problem most of us have is that we create a vision for our lives and focus only on the final destination without considering the steps to get there. What we should do is take one day at a time and place our energy in changing the present circumstance. Your life can shift in an instant because of one opportunity, but you can't bank on random opportunities.

Economies rise and fall, and people change their minds at the drop of a hat. What you can bank on is yourself, because it is your actions that create those serendipitous, wealth-generating moments.

Our brain treats goals like a valued possession, so failing to meet them will trigger feelings of loss, anxiety, fear, and sadness.[5] If you set out to accomplish five things within the same timeframe, each task is only going to get 20% of your attention. Maybe not even that much. Because if you've invested so little of your time in the first place, it makes it that much easier to neglect and forget.

---

[5] Anna Kegler. *RJ Metrics* (2014) *The Psychology of Goal Setting*

BRAIN: You promised me you'd start a business.

YOU: I know but I was hoping to...

BRAIN: You suck, I'm taking back my dopamine.

YOU: Aaarrrrrggghhh *instant migraine*

As incredible as you are at juggling all that you do on a daily basis, it's important to come to terms with the fact that until you make that Oprah-money, you are only one person with finite resources.

Map out one transformational goal. Outline the resources you need along with what you already have to accomplish it. This includes your capabilities, time, money, equipment, and support from other people.

Once you've sifted through everything, create a roadmap to get to your destination. Get laser-focused on accomplishing each task leading up to it for the next 90 days. 90 days is long enough to get your act together and short enough to give you a sense of urgency.

Trying to do everything slows your progress.

Say you want to launch your website. It could be considered to be a transformational goal because it can significantly improve your brand presence. Sure, you could get a template and launch it in a week or two, but if you want to make it into a tangible marketing asset, you'd need considerably more time to work on the copy, design, and other important elements.

From this one goal, you'll work out all that needs to be done to make it da-bomb-dot-com. This includes creating an action list along with specific dates of completion. It's about putting on the blinders, keeping your eye on the prize, and seeing it through to the end.

MAKE MEANINGFUL MICRO-DECISIONS

Before you hit the snooze button, scroll through your email, or check out what Brad's doing on social media, let it be your mission to use those early morning moments to make meaningful micro-decisions. What makes them meaningful is the fact that you know that they contribute to the vision you have of living your best life.

Our brain likes it when we accomplish goals of any kind — no matter the size[6]. It uses it as a reference of our success and thanks us by injecting doses of the happy hormone dopamine into our bloodstream. Therefore, following through on making your bed and meditating before you head downstairs for your caffeine fix puts you in the right frame of mind for slaying bigger tasks.

You need to feel good to make progress. With that said, give yourself grace about what you can actually get done. Life isn't perfect, things come up, you may even fall into old habits — the important thing is to not stay there. Be open to the possibility that circumstances can change, yet determined enough to get back on track.

OPEN YOUR MOUTH

Since you're on a mission to create an awesome website, do the scary thing and tell people about it. Doing this lights a fire under you to make sure that it gets done.

---

[6] Monica Mehta (2013) *Why Our Brains Like Short-Term Goals:* Entrepreneur

Not saying that you need to brag about its awesomeness, the finished product will do that for itself, but tell people about it. Put it on social media, tell your friends and family, even tell some work colleagues. You want to hold yourself accountable. Taking this action opens you up to facing the potential shame of being all talk if your goal wasn't achieved. No one wants that kind of embarrassment.

There are *some* things you want to keep under wraps if you think that being incognito will have a bigger impact. An example of this is working out a partnership with an organization to share your services with the masses. It wouldn't be wise to talk about it until the ink is dry. But in most cases, if you tend to not follow through with your goals, make it a practice to open your mouth.

If you're worried about people taking your ideas, do a quick search on Google. You'll find pages and pages on pretty much the same thing. I remember having an idea for a show featuring underground Caribbean musical artists. I didn't tell anyone about it. But a few weeks later in the newspaper, I saw the same concept from a producer in Europe. It goes to show that great ideas are not confined to our own mind.

Sometimes our ego stops us from getting things done. It may even be due to some superstitious mumbo-jumbo. A client of mine Sara was telling me how she posted a quote on her social media about not telling people your plans so that their energy couldn't ruin it. She got lots of double taps. Mingled between the supportive comments and hand-clapping, one follower's words changed everything:

"I don't agree with this. By believing this, you're opening yourself up to being influenced by other people's energy and not your own. You're giving them the power to put a hex on you and your plans."

Whoa. That's some deep stuff. I don't know about the hex part, but you get the point. Finally seeing the light, she deleted the post.

You have to come to terms with the fact that people will sometimes try to use your ideas. Happens to me all the time. Sure, it can be annoying, especially if it's someone you don't like. But unless it's blatant copyright infringement I wouldn't get too worked up about it. Consider yourself an inspiration. Even Michelangelo studied other artists' work to perfect the statue of David. What you produce is still unique. You are the key component in the equation. There are people out there that need to hear your voice to feel empowered. So open your mouth and don't be afraid to shine.

LEARN FROM SUCCESS

Ever heard of the phrase *"no man is an island"?* Sure you have. But that hasn't stopped you from trying to do it all on your own has it?

When I was starting out, I thought I could do and be everything for my business. Any questions I needed answered could be found on Google. I was all about bootstrapping. Big mistake. If you looked up the word 'exhausted' in the dictionary, you'd see my face. I wasn't willing to invest in myself or trust people. The problem with thinking you can do it all is that you actually end up doing it all, and that limits your potential.

Sometimes we avoid asking for help because it tells our egos that we aren't enough.

When I eventually got fed up with my snails-pace growth, I decided to develop mentoring relationships — ones where I was the mentee and others where I was the mentor. It was scary because mentorship requires vulnerability and opening yourself up to criticism. But I needed results since my way obviously wasn't working.

Hands down, it's one of the best decisions I've ever made. I constantly engage in conversations with people who call me out on my crap while still cheering me on. These people hold me accountable for my goals and remind me to stay focused on my mission.

As it is with most things in life, this wasn't an I-made-a-decision-and-life-was-perfect situation. Not everyone is meant to be your mentor just because you admire them, and not everyone is supposed to be your mentee just because you want to help. I've been burned before where a mentor just wanted to scam my ideas for their personal gain, and I've also supported mentees who didn't want to put the work from my guidance. Both scenarios made me frustrated because I wasted my time. However, persistence is for the strong. I lived in optimism, paid attention to red flags, and made better choices. I even started facilitating my own mastermind sessions because at least I could screen who entered my success circle.

Who can you trust? Who is pushing you forward? How much value do you place on information? If you're tired of doing it on your own and ready to get some clarity on the direction you should take, here are some things to consider when looking to develop a coaching or mentoring relationship:

Book a discovery call: These are 15 - 20 minute conversations where you can get a feel of the person's personality. This is ideal when the person is a professional coach and you can easily track their performance from client testimonials. A good sign that it's the right fit is that you feel energized and inspired at the end of the chat.

Find someone who has been there: If you want to learn how to fish you don't go to a carpenter, right? Do your background checks, ask them where they've been, what makes them an authority, etc. That way you can ensure that they can support you in achieving your ultimate goals.

Asking questions about YOU: A sign of a good coach or mentor is that they want to learn about what makes you tick before starting a relationship. They value their time just as much as you do. They know that in order to create a plan to best support your growth they need to know who you are and where you want to go.

Don't be cheap: When setting up a formal mentoring or coaching relationship it's likely going to come at a fee. There's a strategy behind this. If it's worth anything, it costs something. Come on, did you actually use those free online courses you signed up for? If you paid for them, they probably wouldn't have ended up in your inbox graveyard. We tend to be committed to something when we know we have to fork out some dough, no matter what it is.

Put yourself out there: Most people are willing to offer support if you ask, especially if you can show evidence of how you're making your dreams a reality. We have to remember that mentors are people too. While their time may be limited, it's been my experience that people at the height of their career want to give back as an act of gratitude for their good fortune.

One other thing, please don't run up to people and ask them to be your mentor. It's weird. Learn their story and try as best as possible to model their actions. If you get the chance to meet them, introduce yourself and build from there.

Keep your options open: You can have multiple mentors. It's possible that someone you consider to be an excellent business leader may not be the one you lean on for spiritual guidance, so it makes sense to have a diverse support system.

You should also be open to peer-mentoring. A mentor doesn't have to be older than you, they simply need to have the experience that can support you going to the next level.

NO.

Did you know that *"no"* can be a complete sentence? People pleasing is a disease. Psychologists say that the intense need to please is rooted in rejection[7]. Because we want to be loved and valued, we do what we believe it takes to make that happen. But there are people out there who will manipulate you. People pleasers never get the love and respect they deserve because people see them as weak.

If there's one thing I want you to leave you with, it's the recognition that you have the right to say no without explanation. Doing this lets you stay in

---

[7] Leon F. Seltzer (2002) *From parent-pleasing to people-pleasing:*Psychology Today

your power, preserves your sanity from overcommitting to multiple things, and gives you room to focus on your goals.

CHAPTER FOUR

KNOW WHO YOU WANT TO SERVE

I have a cool friend named Taylor. She's a savvy, soulful, and shrewd millennial. She's all about self-development and is pretty strategic in her approach to getting things done. Taylor is a straight-laced high achiever, but isn't afraid to bust a move when she hears *Thriller* playing.

She likes nice things but isn't superficial. She spends wisely. She only opens her purse for something she knows that will last or help her in the long run.

She's a self-motivated creative. She's a people person, but has strong introverted tendencies. She's a natural leader, even though she struggles with her confidence from time to time. She hates feeling restricted and knows that her purpose in life is to help people using her gifts. But she gets confused at times deciding which gift to serve with. She craves living in her true potential, both professionally and personally.

Does this sound kind of familiar? If it does, it's because Taylor is my ideal client.

I know who she is because I did my research and created a profile. Creating an avatar makes her real to me.

Because I know who Taylor is on a personal level I can figure out how to best serve her. I know her needs, which means that I can pin down messages that resonate with her. When I find myself about to take action, I sometimes say *"No, Taylor wouldn't like that"* or ask *"How would Taylor feel about this?"*.

I tend to have these conversations in private so that my husband doesn't think I'm going off my rocker.

It's important to zone in on who your ideal client is regardless of whether you own a business or work for one. If you own a business, it guides you on how to create products and services that cater to their needs. If you're a professional, it will help you identify the kind of corporate structure where you'll feel most at home. If who you want to serve values innovation, you probably wouldn't want to work for a company that rents video cassettes. It'll drive you crazy.

Here's something you won't hear too often: you can have more than one ideal client. Let's say you're a business coach with different tiers to your offerings, the language you use to captivate potential clients for a 1-day intensive would be different for your 6-month mastermind. Each group would have different pain points and most likely different income levels. But even though that's the case, you should always have your North Star client. This is the person who you feel most connected with and who you can carry on a buyer's journey with your brilliance with each of your offerings. This person is also deeply aware of their pain point and has a strong need for your offering. How you tell your stories should trigger them to take action so that you can be seen the solution.

If you want to craft stories that attract the right people into your life and business, it starts with you. *Who do you want to work with?*

Give a think about these questions to kickstart getting to know your Taylor. Let's call her Jane.

How old is Jane?

Where does she live?

What was her childhood like?

What does she do for a living?

What's her relationship status?

How much does she earn?

Does she have children?

What does she like/dislike?

What are her deepest fears?

Who does she admire?

What does success look like for Jane?

What are her core values?

What websites does she visit regularly?

What would Jane buy from you?

What does she enjoy doing on her down time?

What challenges does Jane experience?

What products does she hate/love?

Which apps are on her mobile phone?

How would she find out about you?

What is she willing to buy at the drop of a hat?

What does she tell herself to get out of not buying something?

What messages does she need to hear to be convinced that your offer is right for them?

Your ideal client is a dynamic individual just like you. The key to letting them know that "you're the one" through storytelling is to address their pain points – the true nature of a problem they're experiencing. The easiest way to determine this is to read between the lines of your ideal client's profile. Based on what you know of Taylor, it's safe to say that one of her pain points is a lack of clarity of her purpose. Now it's my job to share messages through my storytelling on how working with me can address that.

Once you've figured out who you want to work with, you can nail down your special thing — your genius. That one-of-a-kind superpower that lets you do certain things better than almost anyone else and keeps you energized for the long haul.

CHAPTER FIVE

(RE) DISCOVERING YOUR GENIUS

Camille was a born bohemian. She loved to sing, write poetry, and get lost in her grandfather's books about the lives of great people throughout history. It was in those ancient texts that she could envision a different life for herself. She dreamed of travelling the world, having a big family, and owning a multi-million dollar business. It didn't matter that she had to share a bed with her mother at her grandparents' home after her parent's divorce. It didn't matter that she couldn't get violin or gymnastic lessons because the "We can't afford it" song was on constant rotation. She had hope for a bright future. Because like Queen Elizabeth I, Leonardo Da Vinci, and the other exceptional people before her, she knew that she was made for more – the world was hers for the taking.

She would spend summer vacations with her father, that was the agreement her parents made when they split. Like most teenagers, Camille was constantly interrogated about her career path. But when her father asked the question after she completed her first year of high school, she decided to lie. She never made a practice of doing such things, but she realized that every time he asked, there never seemed to be a suitable answer. So instead of telling him that she wanted to be a writer, she decided to take a different course.

"What do you want to be when you grow up?" he said with stern eyes as if accusing her of murder.

"I want to be an archeologist," she said. Camille was pleased with her answer. She figured that the role was prestigious enough for his approval yet didn't stray too far from her natural desire for adventure. Seemed like a plausible choice.

He rolled his eyes. "Don't be silly. How many archeologists do you know? Can you make money from that?!"

She was confused. Obviously she could make money, otherwise why would it be a profession. But daring not to upset him even further, she resorted to her backup, "Well, I was also thinking about being a dentist".

"You got a 76% in science," he said as he held up her report card. "If you can't even get a good grade in that, why do you think you could be a dentist?".

There was no pleasing that man. She hated science so she thought it was a good grade. Camille went to her room feeling crushed.

Suddenly, the world wasn't filled with possibilities. It would be nice to say that she didn't stain her pillow with tears that night; it would be nice to say that her father's opinions didn't chip away at her self-worth; it would be nice to say that she eventually followed her dreams and became a writer...it would be nice to say, but life isn't always a fairytale.

Determined to prove to her father and herself that she actually was smart, and could make copious amounts of money, Camille studied and worked hard over the coming years. Not only did she graduate at the top of her class, she carried home fat paychecks each month from her career in the pharmaceutical industry. On paper, she was a success, but in her heart she knew something was missing. She just couldn't figure out what.

**Don't allow other people's stories
of you define your reality.**

Many of us are living a vegetative existence because we were made to believe that who we are and the gifts we've been given aren't enough. As we get older, the world gets smaller and so do our dreams based on someone else's perception of success. Most of the time those ideas come from people whose opinions we value most, like our parents. We start to make connections of their words to our experiences, which seem to confirm what we've been told as fundamental truths. Thinking that you can only make lots of money from certain professions is one of them.

The fact is, you can make money doing anything. There are millionaire hot-dog cart vendors, and ocean divers who earn 7-figure incomes. Society's success consciousness encompasses having a massive house, driving an expensive car, and having more money in the bank than we know what to do with. What we don't see is the disconnect between doing what we love and being profitable. It's time to break free from that way of thinking. Life goes by in a flash. Now's the time to spend your time doing what brings you insane joy.

YOU ARE A GENIUS. YOU JUST DON'T KNOW IT YET.

How can we measure what makes someone a genius? Sure, if you're a math whiz you can measure that with a standardized test. But what about abstract fields like art? Many would say that Bob Marley and Pablo Picasso were geniuses.

A *genius* is someone with exceptional intellect, creative power or other natural ability. If that's the case, it means that we all have some form of genius inside us.

Just because you're good at something doesn't mean that you're using your genius power. You may be a top-notch salesperson, but you also cook a mean rib-eye steak. You get lost in the symphony of seasonings; grilling is your happy place. People tell you all the time that you ought to open your own restaurant, but you ignore them. Doing it comes so naturally to you, so you never consider making it a career.

What's your genius? You don't want to wake up five years down the road realizing that you're still not where or who you want to be in life. I want you to spend time marinating on these questions:

What sucks less than anything else? Let's be honest. Nothing will be roses and sunshine 24/7 even when you're living in your purpose. So make a list of activities of what would suck less if you had to do it forever.

What do you want to be remembered for? This will provide not only a vision of where you want to be in life, but what gives you joy. If you want to be remembered for it, it's something you value deeply.

What are you uniquely qualified to do? This includes academic qualifications and life skills. If you're great at creating content and it's a self-taught skill make a note of it. If you're great scouting out the best hotels for backpackers because you've travelled the world, that's a qualification. Think outside the box.

Over the next couple of days, think about your answers and see what feels right. Resistance tends to be a sign that you need to focus on something else.

DON'T WASTE BRAIN CELLS TRYING TO BE MEDIOCRE

Once you've discovered your genius power, it's important that you stay in that zone. Self-improvement is great, but why study dancing when you have two left feet? Avoid doing things that steer you away from your raw talent; it's better to invest your time becoming the best at what comes naturally to you than working toward being mediocre at something else.

If you know you're not good at something, get someone else to do it. Where possible, delegate tasks and outsource. My husband handles the operational side of our business because I don't have the patience to comb through documents, meanwhile he loves it. Strange.

It's also important to create systems. For me, this can involve creating a content plan for the month. So instead of wasting my brain cells trying to think of things to post on a whim, I invest my time educating and empowering women to be their best and most profitable selves.

CHAPTER SIX

BATTLING WITH IMPOSTER SYNDROME

Imposter syndrome (noun): chronic self-doubt that makes you feel like you're a fraud; a negative emotional state that overrides any feelings of success despite external proof competence[8].

Angelisa was what you would call a "professional student". She had two degrees, one masters, and was thinking about getting a PhD.

On our first coffee date, she told me about her consulting business. When she mentioned how much she was charging for her services my draw dropped. I couldn't believe how low her rates were. She had the experience, the qualifications, and a market primed to pick her brain. She shrugged off my confusion by saying that she "simply wanted to help" people, which was why she charged so little.

Okkkkkk. Red flag.

---

[8] Gill Corkindale (2008) *Overcoming Imposter Syndrome*: Harvard Business Review

"Besides, this is just my side-hustle. I have a full-time job," she added.

'nother red flag.

Two mochaccinos and one orange muffin later, Angelisa started to open up. I found her to be an extremely intelligent woman, albeit a braggart. I enjoyed hearing about her adventures abroad, and how her innovative strategies saved companies millions. Between the tales of grandeur, she managed to slip in a few complaints about her younger "underqualified" boss who constantly overlooked her "brilliant" ideas.

"Do you know that he never even finished grad school?" she said while rolling her eyes. "He's moving to a new firm next month. I can't wait till he leaves. Good riddance".

"Since you obviously have the goods to do a better job, are you planning on applying for his position?" Angelisa seemed to shrink in her chair when I asked that question.

"No, there's no point," she responded. "I have way too much on my plate to deal with office politics".

There it was, the moment I figured out Angelisa's problem. She was suffering from severe *imposter syndrome*. Most people would have mistaken her borderline conceited persona for confidence. Nope, despite all her achievements, her behaviour told me that she felt like a fraud.

Pushing to reach the pinnacle of your academic career is great, but Angelisa's reason was due to the fact that she didn't feel like she ever knew enough. School was a copout. If she was busy with courses, she would be too busy for anything else. She also used minimizing language to describe her business as "just a side-hustle". She had low fees because she didn't think her services were worth more. After years of complaining about how her boss did things when faced with the opportunity to take control she made excuses why it wasn't the best fit for her. Every action she could take to progress was dead on arrival.

Can you see how Angelisa's imposter syndrome affected her brand? She may have thought that she was presenting herself as a highly educated and confident woman, but because that didn't align with her core beliefs, it muddied up people's perception. Clients would have undervalued her services. At first, her credentials would have made them believe that they hit the jackpot. But since her rates were so low, it would naturally make them wonder if she was as good as they originally thought. As for her boss, the fact that he constantly overlooked her was clearly because of how she engaged with him. If she couldn't contain her disdain for his position with me, it's unlikely she could do it around him.

Angelisa didn't exactly receive my assessment with open arms, but she knew I was right. Several coffee dates later, she came to grips with how she was holding herself back. She increased her consulting rates, and as a result started attracting projects that made her feel energized. She even decided to hold off on getting that PhD and instead confidently served people with the wealth of wisdom she already had. Though her boss ended up staying with the company, she started to build a better relationship with him since envy no longer clouded her judgement. For the first time in a long time, she was genuinely happy and confident.

When you're that much closer to your genius power you may wonder if you're a fake. You start to question if you really have what it takes to put yourself out there, serve your people, and accomplish your dreams.

Newsflash. Everyone feels that way from time to time.

"I have written eleven books, but each time I think, 'uh oh, they're going to find out now. I've run a game on everybody, and they're going to find me out". – Maya Angelou

When those feelings start to creep in, here are some ways you can shut them down:

KEEP YOUR EYE ON THE PRIZE

You have to stop comparing yourself to others and focus on your own goals. Some people may seem more successful than you at the moment, but you have to run your own race. You're also not fighting a fair fight with your self-worth. Everyone has unique experiences that have shaped who they are and have sharpened their abilities. That doesn't make what you know less valuable. Out of the billions of people in the world, there are people who need exactly what you have to offer. Keep your sights on them.

GET STARTED

Aim for progress and not perfection. Start doing things you know will take you to the next level, even if it freaks you out. Taking action provides clarity on your next move because it tells you what not to do and how to do things better.

You won't have all the answers. If you're a spiritual gal like me, you ought to know that God will not roll out the red carpet to the final destination. Otherwise, what's the point of having faith? Tarot cards and all that jazz may seem like a comfort to provide 'answers' but it's really a crutch that only adds to your confusion.

Tyler Perry compares his road to success to walking in the dark, guided by the light of an old cellphone[9]. You know, those early models with the flashlight on top. He could only take small steps at a time because the light could only go so far. It's the same way for everyone else's journey. Take steps of faith with what you already have and see where it takes you.

"Failure is simply the opportunity to begin again, this time more intelligently." – Henry Ford

---

[9] Joel Osteen Radio (2018) *'Higher Is Waiting'* featuring Tyler Perry: YouTube Video

STOP THINKING THINGS HAVE
TO BE DIFFICULT

When what we do seems effortless, we tend to psych ourselves out on using it as a means of generating wealth. The reason for this is because we've tied wealth to work, and work must be unenjoyable, right? No. If that were true Beyoncé would only be singing in her shower instead of packed arenas. What's easy to you may be difficult to someone else. Or maybe they just don't want to bother doing it themselves. Either way, just because what you do comes naturally, doesn't mean that it's not the best thing since sliced bread to someone else.

GIVE YOURSELF SOME PROPS

We can easily forget how far we've come when we're in mission-mode. Always take mental notes of your achievements. Heck, get a gratitude journal and write it down if you need a reminder. You have to programme your mind to accept praise from yourself.

Give yourself some positive self-talk and visualize your success on a daily basis. The brain can't tell the difference between what's real and imagined.

The more you rehearse something in your mind, the easier it is to become habituated in reality.

What also helps is thinking about someone you've supported in the past. You may not feel like who you are or what you do is phenomenal, but the person you helped would disagree. Keep a file of testimonials and check it out from time to time. Be proud of your achievements and thank yourself.

LET YOUR TRIBE GIVE YOU A REALITY CHECK

Your tribe is your people. They're your cheerleaders, your confidants, your tough-love givers. You have different tribes for different needs. Masterminds are geared toward professional development which can have two or more persons. Other tribes can be informal, like online groups of people who have a shared interest, or friends from college that meet once a month for coffee.

A tribe can pop up in unexpected places. This was the case for Shelly at one of my workshops. Shelly had just started her events management company but, like Angelia, was suffering from imposter syndrome. She had just quit her job and was worried about how she was going to make ends meet. She also had her young son to take care of. Shelly was fearful of not getting clients because she was entering an industry that had other big names in the game. She was also worried that people wouldn't hire her because of her lack of academic credentials. As her voice started cracking and tears began to run down her face, she shared that she used her last available cash to come to the event. Whoa. This was a group coaching workshop so it was designed for getting real, but no one, including myself, expected this.

Someone with a PhD only means they spent more years in college than most people. It doesn't make them experts.

Like stormtroopers on a rescue mission, everyone immediately banded together to save Shelly from herself. We drilled down and gave her a reality check. We discovered that she had planned events before so she did have experience. We let her know that having a piece of paper was worth shit in the event planning industry, what mattered was leveraging her reputation from past clients. As for the money, my amazing students let her know that she made the right decision. Because not only was she building connections, she learned insights from other women who were once at rock bottom in the early days of their business and ended up making millions.

When hanging out in a tribe, it's important that their energy and goals are aligned with yours. You can get some great insights from people from all walks of life, but if they don't have a positive outlook or would rather spend their time watching reality shows than building their career, they may not be the best ones to surround yourself with. It's said that there is power in proximity[10]. If you're the sum of the five people you spend the most time with, make sure that they're on your wavelength.

Trust and respect are also crucial factors. People in your tribe should be able to contribute freely without judgement and vice versa. Shelly was lucky to be surrounded by people who had those characteristics. They gave her the reality check she needed which allowed her to get over her insecurities and build a thriving business.

---

[10]Tony Robbins (2020) *Power is Proximity: Why you must surround yourself with people who challenge you*

YOU DON'T NEED TO KNOW EVERYTHING

If you could read people's thoughts, you would realize that every single person doubts their capabilities. Conversely, some people are genuinely oblivious to their ineptitude because they're too incompetent to realise it – otherwise known as the *Dunning-Kruger Effect.*[11] You know, the ones that make you wonder how they manage to tie their shoes let alone run a business. But as Angelisa learned, you have to give them credit. They're getting things done while other people are looking on scratching their heads.

Being plagued with imposter syndrome, is an indication that you do have enough knowledge. You don't need to be lightyears ahead in wisdom to offer support, you just need to be a few steps ahead. You worry because you see every angle. Plus, you actually care about the subject matter and the people you're trying to help. These are all good things. Remind yourself that no one knows everything, and it's better to move forward with what you have than standing still wondering how people less equipped did it.

---

[11] Oliver Burkeman (2014) *Nobody Knows What The Hell They Are Doing*

FACE YOUR MORTALITY

You're going to die. Sorry to get dark, but you need to face this reality. The biggest regret most people have when they're nearing the end is not having taken more risks. Do you want to be on your deathbed with flashbacks of things you should have done because you thought that maybe you weren't ready or good enough? Didn't think so.

CHAPTER SEVEN

YOUR VALUES CREATE VALUE

Pretty much everyone across the globe knows Tiffany & Co. as a prestigious jewelry store. They've existed since 1837, and have been a staple in popular culture ever since.

When you think of the brand, the words *love* and *luxury* tend to come to mind. This is no accident. It's due to decades of positioning.

One day while aimlessly scrolling through my feed, I came across a meme that made me do a double take. It was a photo of a $1,500 platinum paper clip from Tiffanys. The caption read: *...for that price, it better hold my life together.*

I figured the whole thing was a joke, but there it was on the website: Tiffany & Co. was selling paper clips. Go figure. Granted, it's not the kind you use to hold dirty research papers together, but it's a paper clip nonetheless. But you know what, people of various income levels will buy it because it's a *Tiffany Paper Clip*.

If another relatively unknown jewelry store took it up a notch and created a diamond-encrusted platinum paper clip that came with a puppy, it's safe to say that those same people won't be breaking down the door to get it.

Values shouldn't be arbitrary characteristics of your business, they should be intentional.

You need your values to shine throughout your brand because values are what resonates with clients and helps you attract and keep customers. Take for instance Pepsi and Coca Cola. Many blind studies show that most people can't taste the difference between the two sodas.[12] It proves that the deciding factor for them is psychological. It's not only the perception of a difference in taste, it's something more. It's the values assigned to each brand.

Despite being several decades old, Pepsi will always be seen as the new kid on the block compared to Coca Cola. Pepsi values being hip whereas Coca Cola values being classic. They own those values and leverage it to appeal to their target audience.

---

[12] Gus Lubin (2012) *Here's The Real DifferenceBetween Coke And Pepsi*: Business Insider

People will value your brand based on your values. It's the reason why people are die-hard Apple users and some swear by Samsung products. It's why environmentalists will most likely purchase Toyota Prius and people who like high-class rides will get a Mercedes Benz.

COMING FACE TO FACE WITH VALUE CONFLICT

Identifying your core values is more than just picking a few words because they sound good. It's about looking at your history and figuring out why they mean so much. They create a framework for authentic storytelling.

One of the easiest ways to determine your values is to recognize what makes us feel *value conflict*. This is the feeling of extreme negative emotions when having to encounter opposing values. Knowing them will not only help you to get a better understanding of your innate drivers, it will also give you a clearer image of the kinds of clients and businesses you don't want to work with.

Spend some time thinking about what gets you peeved. For example, if *honesty* is a core value, you may feel very upset or uneasy when engaging with dishonest people or hearing stories of corruption. This would mean that you would have a hard time using dishonest tactics to make a sale. Good.

Now it's time to select what you determine to be your top five values. Spend at least 15-20 minutes to think about at least three experiences, from as far back as possible, and the reason why you hold each of these values close to your heart. Take the same steps to identify value at least five value conflict scenarios. Note experiences why you believe you have these strong emotions with as much detail as possible.

CHAPTER EIGHT

YOUR BRAND IS LIKE AN ONION

...it has layers.

Sorry, couldn't think of a sexy fruit with layers.

A pomegranate. Your brand is like a pomegranate. No layers, but you'll see where I'm going with this later on.

Many events have led you to where you are now. You are the sum of those experiences, even the ones that you never gave a second thought. Now that you're on your way to work on your signature story, here are some things to keep in mind:

- Stories are abstract and cross-functional, meaning that they can mean different things to different people.

- Stories reinforce human connections, which is important if you aim to monetize your personal brand.

- Having a signature story significantly boosts your public relations strategy.

- It is medium-agnostic which means that it can be told through blog posts, webinars, infographics, social media advertising, and other forms of content.

THE HOME FOR YOUR SIGNATURE STORY

75% of buyers say that website content influences their buying decision.[13] That's a huge chunk of folks. Truth be told, you don't need a website to run a profitable business. You can easily leverage private groups online once you're engaging the audience. But if you want to scale your brand for the long haul, you ought to have a website.

Here are some other reasons:

- It gives you instant credibility. Major news publications want to see that you have one if they're going to do a feature on you.

- It acts as a marketing medium to showcase your content and signature story.

---

[13] Blue Corona (2018) *Do I need a website for my small business? Yes, you do. Here are 8 reasons why.*

- You don't own your social media pages. If there's an algorithm shift you may not be reaching the same people you did before.

- Your competitors have one. Don't think I need to say more.

- People trust search engines. SEO makes a huge difference in connecting customers to brands. Your website is a hub for keywords relevant to your brand.

There's simply no excuse for not having one. But looking pretty and having great content counts for nothing if one particular section isn't on point.

SPOILER ALERT: IT'S NOT REALLY "ABOUT" YOU

Did you know that the *About Page* is the 2nd-highest visited page behind the homepage? This is because it houses your signature story and tells users what they can expect to find. You want it to do a couple of things:

- get new visitors excited to have found you and want to stick around

- send users to the right place (which can be your lead magnet or services page)

- inspire your target audience to trust you by showing that you're qualified and have a proven track record in your field of expertise

- tell people how they can contact you

There are many creative ways to format this page. Whatever style you go with, you need to make it clear who you serve, what product or service you offer, and what action you want them to take after checking it out. No one wants to read a long, drawn-out biography. Remember to share the most relevant and outstanding information to captivate your target audience.

GREAT STORIES SHOWCASE THE HUMAN CONDITION

Take a moment to think about your favourite movie. One of mine is *Guardians of the Galaxy*.

Without getting too much into the details, it's about an underdog facing an insurmountable situation, who finds the power within himself to rise above it all, while becoming a beacon of hope and badassery.

If this sounds familiar it's because that's the human condition. Most stories, no matter the genre, follow the same patterns and archetypes.

We all face something that seems like it wants to beat us to a pulp. Maybe it's that soul-sucking job that just forces you to venture into having your own business. Or maybe it's an inner conflict where you battle with not using your gifts to serve a greater purpose.

When we hear stories of other people, heroes that rose above it all, we get inspired and believe that it's possible for us too. Stories give us hope for infinite possibilities. It's why people strive toward being more than they are at any given moment, and why movies and books make massive sales.

Crafting your signature story requires taking a stroll down memory lane. Consider it your *origin story* — it shares how it all started, your struggles, when it all took off, and how your transformation gave you the power to serve others with your gifts.

Now that you're up to speed, here's the outline for crafting your *signature story*:

The Monster: What challenge or challenges did you face? This is where you share some background on your character and the circumstances that made you feel uncomfortable.

The Quest: What did you experience along the way? When you faced the challenge, think about the people and places that had an impact on your journey.

The Hero Emerges: What was your coming-of-age moment? Think about the specific point in time where you discovered yourself and decided to take action. It's the moment where you recognize your power to kick that monster in the face.

The Transformation: Describe the triumph after your discovery and the lessons you learned. Share how your journey made you into the amazing human you are today and how you use your newfound superpowers to help others.

CASE STUDY: TOMS SHOES

Blake Mycoskie "witnessed the hardships faced by children growing up without shoes" while traveling in Argentina in 2006. "Wanting to help, he created TOMS Shoes, a company that would match every pair of shoes purchased with a new pair of shoes for a child in need"[14].

Sounds like something you would support, right? Heck yeah. This is a great example of a *signature story pitch*. This is a clear and easily recognizable summary of your brand that tells people in a brief way why they should listen to you.

It has to revolve around a clear mission, something that your target audience can get behind, one that makes them feel inspired, and see the value of what you're doing.

SIGNATURE STORY PITCH

Your audience may not have the time to take in all the juicy tidbits of your origin story, but having a short narrative can encourage them to seek you out and learn more about who you are and what you do.

Your *signature story pitch* must be human, relevant, and interesting. It must also have the following elements:

- who you are

---

[14] Blake Mycoskie (2012) Blake Mycoskie's Bio: TOMS Shoes

- the challenge

- your solution to the problem

- who you serve

- the transformation

If you go back to the case study, you'll see that it has all of the abovementioned elements, and it only took 45 words to get those points across.

The fabulous thing about creating a signature story pitch is that once you've got it down, you will always have something to say when people ask for some backstory on what you do, whether it be for interviews, presentations, or networking events. Here are some best practices:

- Keep it short, no more than 45 seconds.

- Practice saying it in the mirror for flow.

- This should go without saying, but show enthusiasm about your mission.

- Don't lead with a job title, this isn't an elevator pitch.

- Avoid clichéd words and breathless phrases such as "results-driven" or "furiously passionate". Say what feels easy and natural.

MAKE REGULAR DEPOSITS TO YOUR STORY BANK

Your *story bank* is a collection of narratives you can draw on for occasions to build equity for your brand. Even though nailing your signature story is important, you don't want to be a drone telling the same account of your life without including some inflections.

Besides the bonus of adding new angles to your content, you can make withdrawals *shameless pun* from your story bank when you're about to do interviews or when you have to do a speech. The goal is to share narratives that add vantage points to how people see you.

If your signature story revolves around how you used to suffer from major anxiety after the death of a loved one but you found a way to overcome it through holistic wellness practices, you could pull from your story bank a supporting narrative about how you met your partner at a yoga class during that period. By sharing that little sweet seed of information (told you you'd get the pomegranate reference) you added dimension to your brand while still maintaining the big picture of your signature story.

Be sure to make regular deposits *second shameless pun* into your story bank. As you would have learned from the last chapter, reflecting on your values is a great way to discover those stories buried deep inside of you. But another method is simply to commit to journaling every day. Yes, every. single. day. It's either that or tear your hair out each week trying to find new narratives to engage your audience. Just let it all hang out. You can make sense of what you wrote later on. If you had a brilliant idea, got ticked off by the customer service rep at Burger Heaven, rescued a puppy from traffic named Mr. Jingles, write it down.

When you're ready to make sense of what you wrote, make sure that the narratives align with your brand by asking yourself these questions:

- What do I want people to feel when they think of me?

- Will this message resonate with my ideal client?

- How do I add value to every piece of content?

- What action do I want my audience to take?

SAME INGREDIENTS, DIFFERENT COOK

I love my mother-in-law's curried chicken. It's like crack. I don't know what magic she weaves into it because no matter how I try to duplicate it, it never tastes the same. Still stupendous, but not the same. That's how storytelling works. It may have the same structure but the difference is who's telling it.

By the way, I'm so proud of you. Many people don't take the time to discover their story. Now that you've gone through the soul work portion of mastering your message, you're going to learn how to turn those stories into brand assets.

CHAPTER NINE

COPY THAT BRINGS HOME THE BACON

Ever gone on a super hot date and as soon as they open their mouth you run for the hills? Yeah, it's the same way when people visit a great looking website or check out content with poorly written (or straight up boring) copy.

Good copy increases your brand's credibility and likeability. Great copy hits all the sweet spots and grabs the attention of your ideal client for the long haul.

Words are the root of great content — whether you read it, hear it, or see it come alive in video. We can talk about all kinds of creative ways to create and repurpose content, but if you want people to listen, you first have to craft the right words to get their attention.

"IT'S NOT YOU...IT'S YOUR COPY"

Well, maybe no one actually says that, but if your website and blog posts send them straight to snoozeville that's pretty much what they're thinking when they leave...never to return. Kiss that potential customer or opportunity goodbye.

Your copy should act as a powerful word of mouth that attracts your dream clients. You want your audience to connect with your brand in a way that makes them feel that hiring or buying from you is a no-brainer.

Writing brings your stories to life, storytelling makes them immortal.

Even though you got A+ for Literature in high school, you're going to need to refine your writing skills. One clear sign you need help is that your grammar-game is on point but your copy lacks personality. Maybe you need to shake off the professor-tone and loosen up your writing. Another sign is that you're too scared to hit *publish* on your blog or social media post, a lack of confidence is a surefire indication that you need help.

Short of going to college and investing years of your time learning this skill, here are some non-technical best practices to take your copy to the next level:

WRITE HOW YOU SPEAK

You don't want to sound robotic. This is true whether you're sharing content on your website or contributing an article to a major press platform like *Business Insider*.

Writing how you speak makes your words connect with readers because it has a conversational tone. Still, you want to keep your audience in mind. If how you speak in your daily life is a bit too casual and uses one too many jargons, modify your word selection. For instance, if you want your brand to have a straight-laced corporate feel, you might want to say *got to* as opposed to *gotta* in your copy.

The apostrophe is your friend. This little floating line isn't just for showing possession of something, it's also great for *contractions*. Apostrophes in contractions shorten a word and make it less formal. We use contractions in our daily lives which is why it makes copy relatable. Honestly, does anyone say: *They are going to the supermarket*? No. *They're going to the supermarket.*

Part of writing how you speak means talking directly to your audience. Imagine what you would say if the person was a friend sitting right in front of you. Even if you're writing for thousands of people, using pronouns like *you* or *we* throughout your copy engages them — they become part of the story instead of passive listeners.

Once you've written the words, read them out loud. This helps you identify any awkward sentences and punctuation issues. If you want people to hear your voice in their heads, make sure it sounds good in yours first.

DON'T BE OBFUSCATE

Calvin and Hobbes is my favourite childhood comic. It wasn't until I got older that I realized that it was really for adults. It was simple, light-hearted, funny copy. But every now and then, my 7 year old self would see a word like *arbitrary* or *sycophant* that perked up my pigtails. It was a good thing. It helped my vocabulary because I had to run for the dictionary. There has to be a balance. Don't confuse readers by going on a long-winded literary trail. Unless you're writing an academic paper, keep fancy words to a minimum.

"If you can't explain it simply, you don't understand it well enough." – Albert Einstein

There's something to be said for keeping things simple. Remember that teacher who would spend the entire class trying to drill a new concept into everyone's heads? Mine was Ms. Gilbert. She would take you around the world and back again explaining the intricacies of osmosis, then get mad when everyone didn't get it. The only way to pass her class was to ask Mr. Wodsworth, the head of the science department. He was direct, didn't spend too much time talking about things that weren't relevant to our tests, and more importantly, he explained things simply. The same rules apply for copywriting. As experts, we can sometimes get so caught up with sharing what we know that we end up rambling. If you want to captivate people, confusing them with every bit of information isn't the way to go.

EXCITE THE SENSES

As his prickly beard grazed her cheek, her body became motionless, but her thoughts were running a mile a minute. With her eyes closed, all she could do was take in the musk scent of his cologne, the firm grip of his strong hands on her waist, and...

Wooo, kinda getting steamy 'round here. While you don't need to channel your inner Danielle Steele with your storytelling, I want you to see how important it is to create an experience for your audience. People want to be able to see, feel, hear and taste your words. Add colour to your copy by being descriptive. Good writers tend to use quite a bit of adjectives to appeal to readers' senses.

ORIGINAL SENTENCE: A lady came asking for Jane.

NON-BORING SENTENCE: A short and fat lady wearing an old brown uniform came asking for Jane.

But how much is too much? Mark Twain's rule for adjectives was *"when in doubt, strike it out"*. If it doesn't add something to the sentence, leave it out or add a supporting sentence.

ALTERNATIVE SENTENCE(S): A short and fat lady came asking for Jane. She was wearing an old brown uniform.

SHARE RELATABLE EXPERIENCES

If your ideal client is a startup mompreneur, boasting about how you're living the single life and spending $5,000 on a Fendi purse isn't likely going to stir good feelings. See life from their perspective. If late nights fueled by coffee and big dreams will resonate with them, tell a tale about that.

Not all stories have to be your own. Maybe the story about a client you served would best suit the message you want to communicate. Make it real for your audience by including details, like your client's name, personality, and feelings. People will still connect with what you're saying because you're the one saying it.

PROOFREID. PRUUFREED. PROOFREAD

There's a reason why writers hire professional proofreaders. It's one of the main reasons why journalists have editors. You can be so intimately involved with your work that you miss obvious grammatical and spelling errors. I once misspelled my own name and didn't see the goof until a few days after someone pointed it out. Geeze.

Copy with these kinds of errors may be overlooked once or twice, but consistent errors make you look like an amateur. Trust me, you don't want to be visited by the Grammar Police (which seems to be everyone on the internet).

Short of having someone read over every bit of work you create, take frequent breaks to see your writing with a fresh perspective. This can be a few hours to a few days. Or better yet, take a long nap to rest your brain.

TELL THEM SOMETHING THEY DON'T KNOW

Fun Fact: If you tell someone that something is a fact, 1 out of 5 people will believe it 100% of the time.

Ok, so that's not actually true. But sharing facts and figures makes whatever you're saying more credible. With so many advertisers vying for our attention with fluffy emotional marketing, cold hard facts appeal to our rational sensibility. It tells people that you valued them enough to do research.

STOP SHOUTING!

Ah, the ubiquitous exclamation sign. This seems to be the most popular form of punctuation. It communicates excitement, or the rantings of a crazy person. Using it too often or multiple times in a sequence can be overkill. It makes you seem disingenuous.

Is what you're saying really warranted that cause of excitement? People need to know when you really mean something. Only use exclamation signs to reinforce an idea and when there's actually something phenomenal to scream about.

ASK QUESTIONS

Give your audience something to think about. Asking questions makes them pause to digest what they've read and work out their emotions. Questions you ask should fall within these categories:

PROBLEM IDENTIFICATION: Wouldn't it be great to not cook dinner after work?

PROBLEM AGITATION: Don't you wish you could take a nap instead of toiling over a hot stove?

SOLUTION QUESTION: Can you imagine how relaxing evenings would be if you had ABC Product?

You don't need to include every kind of question in your copy. There are times when one can make a major impact. But if you're writing long-form copy, space them out. Getting hit with questions back to back can sometimes come off as a cheap emotional ploy.

NOBODY LIKES A SALES STALKER

Don't you hate it when you subscribe to someone's newsletter and then all you get are sales emails? Your subscribers don't like it either.

It's like walking into a store where all you want to do is browse. You have an interest in the products, but you're just not ready to purchase. Maybe you'd do it another day.

Then in 30 seconds flat, an overly friendly sales clerk offers her assistance. You tell her that you're just looking around, but then she keeps trailing behind you like a stalker. She asks if you need help whenever you glance at something. She even tells you about the thread count on a skirt you picked up. Oog. Two minutes later you make a dash for the door. Or in the case of a newsletter, you unsubscribe.

You should give at least 80% worth of value-based content to your audience before sharing any offering. It's like going on two dates then expecting a smooch. Avoid being shut down by letting them get to know you're the best option over time.

SHARE YOUR OFFERING LIKE A NINJA

Now, obviously there are times when you have to send out sales copy. Giving people tidbits over time inside your regular emails and social media posts is a great strategy.

Don't make your offering the main attraction, you want to build excitement for its pending arrival. After generating sufficient interest, drive it home with a call-to-action that allows people to opt-in to receive more details about the offer. See what you did? You gave them the chance to decide if they wanted more information without breathing down their necks. People are more receptive to things when you empower them to choose.

INVITE THEM FOR A SECOND DATE

Imagine spending the evening with a handsome stranger while on your vacation in Spain. He's smart, funny, and seems to be everything you've ever dreamed about. After spending hours exchanging heartfelt stories, he looks deep into your eyes and says "Ok, nice meeting you" and walks away. What the hell?! He was the whole package and now he's gone, gone forever.

So you've written great copy, now what? Don't leave your audience hanging. If they want more, invite them to get more. Tell them how they can access more of your content by including call-to-actions. Think of these as mini commands, all roads lead to this one thing you want them to do.

Created a video about personal branding? Tell people how to access your services. Wrote a guest post about self-care for working moms? Show them that they can learn more on your website. Give people the opportunity to take the next step with you.

Your call-to-action should be concise and relevant to what you're talking about. It should also showcase the benefit of following through. Time-sensitive words and phrases are effective to encourage people to take immediate action like: *Subscribe to my newsletter today for more workplace wellness content.*

GRAB THEIR ATTENTION WITH A CAPTIVATING HEADLINE

It's about persuasion, baby. Creating great content is a gargantuan waste of time if nobody reads it. When people see your headline, you need them to think: *Yeah, this is for me.*

I hate to break it to you, but there's no magic formula for creating headlines. However, what works is to keep in mind the *who, what, where, when, why,* and *how* elements of journalism. Try to work in at least two of the most outstanding parts of the story.

Who are the people involved?
What is this story about?
Where is this happening?
When did it happen?
Why is your story important right now?

How did it happen?

So if the man bit a dog at Union Square last Friday because he was hopped up on drugs during an animal rights rally, the most interesting elements would be the *who, what,* and *when.* Therefore, my headline would be *"Man bites dog during animal rights rally".*

Your copy shouldn't make people scratch their heads; give the people what they expect.

Don't be sensational or deceptive. Give people what they expect. Sensational headlines may get someone to view your copy, but it won't get them to stick around. It's like signing up for those annoying webinars where someone promises to teach you how they scaled their business to 7-figures, which turns out to be a 20-minute money mindset meditation. From the headline down, your audience should know what they're getting when they consume your content.

COPYWRITING IS A MIXTURE OF ART AND SCIENCE

You have to inject your soul into writing while keeping in mind that your copy has a specific mission. This willingness to expose yourself through words is the starting point for connecting with your audience.

Think of some of your favorite writers, it doesn't matter if they write books, movie scripts, or landing pages. Why do you like them? As you grow as a strategic storyteller, it helps to explore other writing styles. Determine what makes these writers effective in bringing their points across, note how they structure their sentences, and see how you can apply some of their techniques and make them your own.

Here's a little assignment for you. Find a few blogs and online magazines that take contributed articles or guest posts. Some of my favourites are *Caribbean POSH*, *Entrepreneur*, *Buzzfeed*, *Disfunkshion* and *Wonder Forest*. Once you've determined which ones are a good fit, get cracking on sharing thought-leadership content. Not only will you improve your writing, you're also extending the reach of your brand.

CHAPTER TEN

FLEX YOUR STORYTELLING MUSCLES

We don't value what we can't see. People wonder why the Kardashians are so popular; it's a running joke that they're famous for doing nothing. But they're superpower is notoriety. They're freakin' everywhere. They leverage people's interest into sales for their products and brand endorsements.

Maybe you're not interested in selling a product or service. Maybe you just want to attract career opportunities. Not tootin' my horn, but I'm a magnet for those. It's not unusual to open my inbox and see an email from someone requesting to work with me, or getting a love note from someone who listens to *The Digital Boss Babe Podcast*.

Posting on social media and hoping for the best is not a strategy. There will always be new trends in content development and digital marketing. Instead of being slaves to algorithms and taking the long road of building your brand, you ought to spend your time refining your magnetic message and sharing it in places where it will have the most impact.

MAGNETIZE YOUR MESSAGE
WITH MASS MEDIA

Want to be featured alongside the big dogs? Heck yeah you do. There's a prestige that accompanies someone's brand when you notice that they've been featured in certain shows or news publications. You think *"Oooo, they must be a big deal if they were in Forbes"*.

...and you'd be right.

One of your major stakeholders in brand building are journalists and new media creators. Besides notoriety, sharing your stories and expertise with the media opens the door for steady streams of traffic and attention — things you need if you want to grow your brand fast.

If you haven't realized by now, I believe in working smart and not hard. Why spend most of your time creating amazing content exclusively for your website and social media pages when you can write a guest blog post for a popular online platform, or simply do an interview and let someone else create the content for you? Plus, you can repurpose those features by sharing it on your channels. Boom (that was the sound of your mind being blown).

SHOW 'EM YOUR OPEN FOR BUSINESS

Speaking of tootin' one's horn, you ought to start doing that on your *press page* if you want to attract media opportunities.

Journalists are always searching the internet for experts to interview. Everyone knows how important it is to have a good looking website and consistent quality content on social media, but what most don't know is that having a press page opens the door for journalists to promote your brand for you. Seeing a press page tells them that you're a serious professional who can drop knowledge at a moment's notice.

Also known as a *digital media room*, the objective of a press page is to anticipate a journalist's information and content needs. While there's no one-size-fits-all format, here are some essential elements:

Company Overview/Professional Bio: Share a short (150 - 250 words) and/or long (300 - 700 words) professional biography. Stick to the important points. Imagine what you would want someone to read if they were introducing you at an event. Mention relevant awards, academic credentials, as well as any involvement you may have in non-profit or charity work.

Approved Images: These would be 3 - 5 high-res professional photographs of yourself. This can include headshots, full-length portraits, as well as behind the scenes photos from speaking engagements. If you don't own the rights to the images, take these steps:

- contact the owner (this is usually the photographer)

- get their permission to place on your page and advise them of the possibility of mass reproduction

- credit the photo to the owner under the image e.g. *Photographer: Kevin Riley*

- make a public note on your page asking that anyone who uses the image credit the owner

Here's an example of what this would look like.

You are free to use these photos with our permission as long as you credit the photographer and send us a link at hello@gizelleriley.com to where they are being used.

Graphics: If you have one, include your brand's logo in a printable resolution. If you're a blogger, a screenshot of your website's homepage is a good option.

Video & Audio Clips: Select a few video and audio clips where you're sharing your expertise. Think of it as evidence that reassures journalists you can handle being interviewed.

Statistics: This is an optional element that's best suited for bloggers and anyone running an online business. Such statistics would include your number of website page views per month and traffic sources, as well as the number of subscribers to your mailing list.

If you're just starting out and your numbers aren't impressive, you can share your growth trends e.g. 800% increase in readership within the past 30 days.

If you have a brick and mortar business, you can feature the demographics of your audience, the number of followers you have on your social media pages, or any other noteworthy statistics.

Testimonials: It's a nice touch to include 1 - 3 powerful testimonials as proof of your brand's greatness. You can request these from past clients, use screenshots from your social media pages, or share a quote from an industry leader who has endorsed you. Select your best ones. Journalists will sometimes attribute direct quotes from these because it saves them from having to reach out to people or coordinate an interview.

Press Library: This section lists your media mentions. Choose 5 - 10 of your most recent and relevant mentions, along with press releases. You can also include a link to another page that shows your entire list of features.

Speaking Topics: You can tell journalists exactly what you want to talk about. Just because your brand revolves around empowering women in business, doesn't mean you want to give them relationship advice. Point out between 3 - 5 specific topics. So instead of a topic being *"women leadership development"*, it may be *"How women CEOs can empower a leadership culture in the workplace"*.

Contact Information: Outline the next steps of how they can get in touch with you with a call-to-action phrase like *click here for booking*. Another option is to include an email address along with the name of your press representative (even if that's you).

Don't give journalists the task of digging. Make sure that your press page is easy to find on your website. You can include links in your *about* page, *home* page, and even your *contact* page. But short of all that, strategic placement would be in your *navigation menu* right after the *about* or *contact* page section since those tend to be high traffic areas.

"HELP! I'VE NEVER BEEN FEATURED!"

Now you're probably wondering what's the point of all this if you've never been scooped by the press. You can still capture golden opportunities by including the essentials, which include your:

- Company Overview/Professional Bio

- Approved Images

- Speaking Topics

- Contact Information

When you've created your amazing page, take it a step further and turn it into a PDF document. This will be your tool to garner attention from potential sponsors and new media creators. You probably haven't realized this, but most of the content we consume doesn't actually come from major news outlets. Every day we're checking out blog posts, podcast episodes, video streams, you name it. The people behind these kinds of new media content are the ones you need to get in touch with to build your brand fast. They dominate niche markets and tend to have a highly engaged audience. This means you can share your expertise on their platforms in order to attract leads for your business.

The barrier to connection is pretty slim. Simply check out their website for a contact email. Sending a simple email letting them know you're available to share your wisdom with their network is enough. When people send me this document asking to be on *The Digital Boss Babe Podcast*, 99% of the time they're going to get an interview because they're prepared. It makes life easier for both of us. Make it attractive so that people would want to take the time to read through it, and make it no longer than three pages.

Once you've booked an interview, determine what you want people to take away from your feature and start pulling narratives from your story bank. Where possible, see if you can get the questions ahead of time. This way you can prepare and rehearse. Regardless if you can or can't get them, brainstorm the questions on your own and watch/listen to past episodes to get an idea of what's coming.

Remember when I spoke about working smart and not hard? There are online services you can use to get contacts and build relationships with the media once you position yourself as a source of information. *HelpAReporterOut* (HARO) helps reporters from global publications who are looking for contributions to beef up their stories. These can be quotes and case studies from the public on particular issues. Email notifications are issued several times a day. If you find a topic you'd like to add your two cents on, act fast and share with the reporter making the request.

CRAFTING CAPTIVATING PRESS RELEASES

Sharing stories in press releases are highly effective. There's just something about issuing and promoting a press release that positions you as an instant authority. Normally used for breaking news, this powerful press tool shares pertinent details of a newsworthy situation written in the form of a super-short story.

Stories can cover the announcement of a new product, a joint venture, events, speaking engagements, philanthropic activities like volunteer work or donations, or new partnerships.

It can be used in a variety of ways even after it's published. You can repurpose it as a blog post, use content as reference material for a book, share an excerpt of a quote on social media, you can even use some core areas as discussion points in a webinar or presentation.

There are many ways to format a press release. We won't get into the layout because frankly, though important, what makes a story get covered is the content. So with that said, here are some tips for writing a press release that the media actually want:

- ensure that the story is newsworthy

- cover the *who, what, where, when, why,* and *how* elements

- have an interesting headline and use no more than 40 characters

- get to the point in the first paragraph

- use at least 1 - 2 quotes to tell the story

- write no more than 2 pages per release

When writing your press release, write like a journalist. This means writing in the third person with a professional tone. This increases your chances of getting coverage. It's like you've given journalists a prepackaged story, plus you've reduced the time it would take them to edit.

As often as possible, share photographs with your press release. Articles with visual content get 94% more readership and exposure than those with copy alone.[15] Our brains are hardwired for images; we used to draw on caves long before we created the alphabet. Photos give the media incentive to cover your story because they have something they can use in case their editor nixes an entire article. It's better that your stories appear as a captioned photograph rather than not getting featured at all.

Send 1 - 3 photos as an attachment with your press release and label them accordingly. For photos with multiple people, add a caption by listing the people in your shot and any other relevant details. Another thing, don't send overly branded photos. Too many logos in the

---

[15] Jeff Bullas (2019) *6 Powerful Reasons Why you Should include Images in your Marketing*

background is a turn-off and because it looks like a cheap promotional ploy.

MAKE SURE YOUR STORIES ARE NEWSWORTHY

"Hey Gizelle, we're about to sign another partnership agreement with XYZ. Can we get some press for this?"

"Another agreement? When was the first one?"

"Last year."

"Is there anything different or special about this one?"

"No, it's just a renewal."

"So, how is it a big deal for right now? Is there something currently happening in your industry that we can associate it with?"

"No. But I figured since we got press for the first one, we can get some more this time around."

No matter how great your brand is, not every activity is considered *newsworthy*. I saved talking about this last because it's so important. It doesn't make sense to share stories that will end up in the trash. It's frustrating for you because you've worked on a story that doesn't get coverage, and to journalists too because you've wasted their precious time reviewing something they can't use. If you want to increase your chances of being scooped, ensure that it has the following elements:

Timeliness: Is it a new story? If it happened a few weeks prior it may be considered as stale news.

Proximity: Does the story apply to members of your community? People are interested in stories happening in their own backyard.

Impact: Does your story matter in the grander scheme of things? Is there a human interest element to the piece? Your stories shouldn't be self-serving.

Novelty: Is your story unusual? *"Dog bites man"* is not as unusual as a *"Man bites dog"* story.

Prominence: Does your story feature celebrities or prominent members of society? A word of caution, you have to carefully consider who you mention since you don't want an unfavorable character to be aligned with your brand.

Journalists have to be ethical and give coverage to stories based on its newsworthiness. But with the influx of pitches they get each day, having a direct contact helps with getting your story seen sooner rather than later.

Call local media houses: If you call and ask for the news editor's email address you'll likely get it. I suggest learning the names of journalists who write stories aligned with your industry. Once you know that, you can ask for their email armed with a name and background information.

Leverage your alumni network: The people you went to school with are sure to know (or even be) a journalist. Ask around or check out their professional history on places like LinkedIn. Though you should be able to get their contact information online, see if you can set up a casual meeting. Outside of media relations, it's a great way to catch up with old friends and make new ones.

Follow them on social media. Join groups where media professionals hang out. Be sure to have a voice and engage with their content by dropping the occasional comment. Eventually, your name will be a common fixture in their mind, so it won't seem odd when you reach out to them because you both share genuine common interests.

Journalists get hundreds, sometimes thousands, of tips for stories each day. You want to provide them with relevant and exclusive content when necessary. Share press releases no more than 1 - 2 times per month. It depends on the type of publication and what day your target audience mostly consumes the content, but I suggest sharing releases on a Thursday or Friday evening as journalists will likely place it in rotation for the weekend.

CHAPTER ELEVEN

HERMITS DON'T MAKE AN IMPACT

Whether you're an introvert, extrovert, or a porcupine (maybe not a porcupine) you *need* people.

Relationships are essential for growing your brand and business, online or otherwise. I'm not talking about the general we-should-meet-up-for-lunch-but-never-do kind of relationships. I'm talking about the ones where after each meeting you both feel compelled to tell the world about this amazing human. Ones that make you feel comfortable enough to casually check in to see how everything's hanging. Ones that when a door of opportunity opens, you're top of mind to be pushed through. Those kinds of relationships.

I love people. Always have. I like hearing their stories and figuring out what makes them tick. But back in the very early days of my career, I was more awkward than anything else. I danced between the extremes of being super quiet or over the top with some goofy, unintentional antic. I simply didn't know what to do with myself.

THEM: Hey, how did you like the presentation?

ME: I see you too are wearing a shirt.

THEM: *backs away slowly*

I used to dream of working from home. I wanted limited interaction with the outside world to avoid the anxiety that came with engagement. But I also wanted to make a massive impact. What can I say, I was a confusing gal.

After years of stagnation, I realized that I had to get over my irrational fear of looking like a fool and y'know...be a functional human. Now I get calls and emails on a regular basis with requests to give my two cents in media interviews and other events. Totally bananas. Don't get me wrong, I still have my fair share of what-the-hell-did-I-just-say moments. This difference now is that I embrace that side of me, she's funny. Something to note, you're only as weird as you think you are. You're not the first person to make mistakes and you won't be the last – it's about progress over perfection.

George R.R. Martin is the novelist responsible for a little series called *Game of Thrones* and a famous introvert. Imagine if he continued writing phenomenal books, but instead of engaging with people to get it out to the masses, he decided to leave it on his desk while it gathered dust. Doesn't make sense right? Nope.

The world needs your gift, but what *you* need is people who are fired up by your mission to share it.

CHAPTER TWELVE

THEY HEARD IT THROUGH THE GRAPEVINE

Do you know the saying *"the fish rots from the head"*?

I first heard it while watching an episode of *Scandal*. Olivia Pope ripped President Fitz a new one for the bad behaviour of his secret service agents — they had a wild night with a bunch of prostitutes that ended in murder. At the time, Fitz was whoring around with pretty much every woman that breathed in a futile attempt to get over Olivia.

It was a good one. You should totally watch it.

So, the decomposition of a fish technically starts from its guts and not the head. I checked. Nonetheless, the message behind those six words always stuck with me.

PEOPLE ARE WATCHING

How many times have you visited an office and the energy is get-me-the-hell-out-of-here? You then meet the CEO and it becomes clear why the air is so thick with coffee and despair. Even if they put on a good face for your benefit, your gut tells you that this person just isn't the real deal. Shady people do shady things. If you're around someone with that kind of energy for 8 hours a day 5 days a week, you're bound to be disgruntled too.

Your actions set the tone for your followers.

On another day, you step into an office where productivity is through the roof. You're greeted with genuine smiles and witness people engaging in playful banter. As you start to question the reality of the space, you spot the boss by the vending machine having a laugh with what looks like a senior executive and two interns. The difference is clear.

SUCCESS (AND FAILURE) LEAVES CLUES

If history has taught us anything, it's that the failure or success of a business starts from the top. Think about it. Bill Gates, Oprah, Richard Branson, Tony Robbins and so many others have tackled some serious setbacks and challenges but still managed to come out on the other side better than ever. They each have a people-centric approach, which is a calling card of magnetic leaders.

There are many reasons why a business could go under — factors like inefficient systems, bankruptcy, and bad management tend to be the major ones. Each seems like plausible reasons, but when you take a deeper look it's really just an excuse for poor leadership. If a problem is recognized before the crap hits the proverbial fan, getting someone else to take over may be the best bet. Companies who were on the brink of disaster like Apple, Yahoo, and Marvel Studios[16] are prime examples that turned things around by changing leadership.

Think of yourself as the captain of the ship. As captain, you have to be able to chart the right course and inspire support from your team to get to your destination. People don't care about the storm. They care how you navigate. Ride that hurricane, baby.

---

[16] Stephanie Vozza (2013) *10 Inspirational Leaders Who Turned Around Their Companies*: Entrepreneur

ARE YOU A GREEN OR RIPE MANGO?

There's an old Jamaican proverb that says *"people don't throw stones at green mangoes"*. It means that people only talk about or attack your character if you've got something going on — you're valuable like a ripe juicy mango on a warm spring day. Mmmm.

I spent my morning commute venting to my taxi driver buddy George. I was going on about how I wish people would take my name out of their mouths. I had a short fuse back then. I don't even remember exactly what it was that got me so upset. What I do remember is that I was overreacting about some speculation about my personal life, which I got wind of when I returned from vacation. After about 10 minutes of passionate rants, George put it in perspective with the green mango adage. I had no real reason to be upset, it was flattering. Clearly, I was important.

If your presence or absence draws attention you have influence. Which means you can naturally expect chatter about you around the water cooler. I was raised to ignore what people said about me. I agree to an extent. I believe that you ought to have a fair idea of what people are saying to see if what they're saying matches with who you are — your personal brand.

You are the CEO of your life. You don't need a fancy title to be a leader, you need influence.

Think of the people you work with as brand ambassadors. They spread the message of your brand at work, at home with their partner, even on social media. If you're going to be talked about, it might as well revolve around the attributes that make you a ripe mango. Not everything you hear will be constructive. Some people have their own agendas or simply like to gossip. Nonetheless, it makes sense to keep your ear to the pavement and filter what you know isn't conducive to your development.

WHO ARE YOU, AND WHY SHOULD ANYONE CARE?

CEOs can easily lose their authority if they fail to control the narrative of their personal brand. You wouldn't believe how many of them make this mistake. Most find it unnecessary. Oftentimes, they suffer from inflated egos, they feel that they've reached the pinnacle of their career so why bother. On the other hand, some could blame it on ignorance since many weren't coached on the art and importance of message mastery.

While you can't control the myriad of thoughts and conversations anyone can have about you, almost like magic, you can shut down the ones that don't align with your brand with your unshakable reputation. Like when the new girl Kristi told Sharon and Natalie that she thinks you're a dictator. They let her know that you're just really passionate about your job because of XYZ. That's what it means to control the narrative. This is the result of message mastery and sharing your personal stories, ones that connect with others in a way where they can't help but spread the word about who you are.

DO YOU REPEL OR ATTRACT?

Actions speak louder than words. Your demeanour is a big part of what colours people's impression. It's a major reason why some organizations attract and retain certain types of employees. As CEOs set the tone for the organization's culture, it's crucial for them to be aware of the messages they're sending out.

Many individuals have wanted to work for a firm simply because of the benevolent and innovative qualities displayed by its leader. Yes, first impressions count, but what sticks is what happens when the honeymoon phase is over. A once energized employee can become despondent because the person's brand that once inspired them turned out to be a facade.

I remember working for a company that had a seriously high turnover rate. We're talking hiring and firing two new people every other month. I should have picked up on the energy in the office, seen the many empty desks, and noted the fact that the CEO was over an hour late for our first meeting. When we finally did meet I was blown away. I thought I was in the presence of a visionary and was baited hook line and sinker. Eventually it was evident that they didn't really care for their employees or customers — it was all about that dollar bill. I fired that job because of value conflict, obviously.

No one will respect you unless they can see who you really are. Authenticity is the cornerstone of trust. Being consistent with your brand means being true to yourself, keeping your word, and being transparent about your actions. Most people would sooner work for a tyrant who is consistent in their behaviour than someone who says one thing then does another.

Do you have favourites? Everyone does. It's the reason why you got that extra cookie from grandma for dessert over your brother. You have to be objective in business. Not just because it lets your team see that you lead with integrity, but because it's simply the smart thing to do. Giving a promotion to the office gossip simply because they stroke your ego is not a good move. Rewarding the right people, whether it be with a compliment, promotion or bonus, sends the message that you're fair and that good work gets rewarded. This inevitably makes people work harder because they know that they'll reap the rewards.

EMPOWER AN ARMY OF STORYTELLERS

You have to clear away any confusion about who you are and how you provide value. Whether you realize it or not, you're empowering an army of storytellers. How you present yourself is the difference between them going to battle for you or preparing for a coup.

There's a whole world of people craving inspiration. The way to get them to champion your message is to be the personification of your core values. Simple. People remember values even if they forget your story. Within the office environment, universally admired ones are *integrity* and *hard work*.

"Katrina's been working overtime to make sure that the elderly couple gets their pension. How nice."

"Wow, I can't believe Katrina stood up to the Dane for picking on Clare. She's badass."

"Did you hear how Katrina raised $300,000 for the company? Whoa, she's got skills."

Showing your colours will encourage people to want to get to know you, so be prepared to talk about your journey. As flattering as it is to have someone ask for your story, think before you speak. You don't want to be pulling things from your story bank willy-nilly. Question yourself to determine if the narrative you're about to share aligns with the brand you're creating. For instance, don't talk about your marital problems or how hard it is to do your job. No. One. Cares. Everyone will see you as a whiner and slowly begin to lose respect. Though you may get some sympathy, oversharing reduces the esteem that automatically accompanies your title or leadership identity.

Engage brain before mouth. Sharing is caring, but not if it makes things awkward.

While it's good to let colleagues see your soft side, do it appropriately and in small doses. Here are some things to think about before you start offloading:

- Does the story have a positive outcome?

- What did you learn from it?

- How can you tailor your communications based on who you're talking with for maximum impact — not all stories are meant for everyone.

Part of stepping into your power is taking a proactive approach to building your army. You want people to see you as a leader. Ever notice how most people want to be *the* leader as opposed to a leader? They spend so much time bitchin' about others and striving for big kahuna roles that they neglect being a person of influence in their present situation. Funny enough, it's the ownership of personal power within the now that makes them elevate to new levels. Here are some ways you can do that while building a culture of open communication within the workplace:

Discuss important issues that don't get enough attention. You can do this in team meetings but it helps to follow up on a one-on-one basis. Keep these sessions informal. You want to make people feel comfortable to share. Make sure to keep sensitive information confidential, otherwise you're basically telling them you're a spy. Being bold enough to unite everyone and lead the conversation positions you as a solution-oriented change-maker.

Work together on planning out of office events. Strategy sessions for deciding the fate of a project is great for cultivating a shared vision, but to create the true spirit of teamwork, you need to get out of the office. Everyone wants to laugh and have fun. Consistently planning events together opens the floor for people to share their whole selves. Oh, please don't call it a "team building" activity, unless it's your intention to host an empty happy-hour. It's a restrictive term that makes it feel like an obligation rather than an option.

Organize office masterminds. Bonds are created when there's trust. It's not easy to get people to spill the beans on things that matter to them. But given some time and the right environment, it is possible. Bring people together to work on personal projects. Give everyone the opportunity to share their goals in a supportive environment, while allowing colleagues to contribute the next steps based on their expertise. The objective is to have everyone walk away after each session with nuggets of wisdom and a plan of action.

CHAPTER THIRTEEN

GET PEOPLE TO LIKE YOU IN 15 MINUTES (OR LESS)

Whether we care to admit it or not, we all want to be liked. Being liked obviously has its advantages. You get invited to parties, ace the interview, close business deals over mimosas, forge friendships — the benefits are limitless.

Science says that people judge our character within 0.1 of a second[17] based on a multitude of unconscious body signals. Here's some great news, what really drives what people think of us is the *second* first impression. The moment you actually *engage*. It's been my experience that all you really need is 15 minutes (or less) to make a killer second first impression.

NO ONE IS BORN MAGNETIC

Some people seem to get along with everyone. My husband Kevin is one of them. Whether he's giving you tough love about maximizing your

---

[17] Jessica Stillman. *INC Magazine* (2016) *People Judge Your Character in 0.1 Second, According to Science*

potential, cracking jokes about your duck walk, or finally taking out the trash (after you've asked three times), you can't help but adore him. But if you ask him the secret behind his charismatic superpower, he'll tell you that he doesn't know.

No one is born magnetic, it's a learned skill. Some acquire it due to their upbringing, and others get it through conscious study. Kevin likely developed his social aptitude during his youth being one of six children in an otherwise large family of aunties and cousins. He also had to engage with people from all walks of life when he would spend his evenings after school working at his grandparent's wholesale shop. He doesn't speak very much, but he's an exceptional communicator. That's because the techniques for cultivating authentic connections have been embedded in his subconscious.

THE PSYCHOLOGY OF BEING LIKED

Growing up, I was always fascinated with how people think and what influenced their behaviour. I read books that most teenagers would probably shy away from, such as *How To Win Friends and Influence People*, *The Definitive Book of Body Language*, Sun Tzu's *The Art of War*, and my personal favorite, *The 48 Laws of Power*. After a while, the lessons I learned from these books, my training as a master neuro-linguistic practitioner, and general observation of other great communicators, wove its way into my psyche. Consider this as your crash course on influence.

GIVE A FIRM HANDSHAKE

Handshakes matter. Here's a little history for you, the ancient Greeks used handshakes as a symbol of trust because it showed that neither person was carrying a weapon. Today, handshakes are seen as a professional act of politeness. Either way, you're basically telling the other person that you come in peace.

Have you ever received a sloppy or soft handshake? Gross. Didn't it give you a less than favourable impression of the person? People judge the kind of person you are based on your handshake, so it makes sense to give a solid one. You don't want to be holding the other person's hand longer than you need to, a one-two pump is enough. Anything beyond that screams *let go of my hand weirdo*.

You can practice with your friends and family to perfect the grip, but a trick you can use is to imagine holding a baby – if it's too loose you'll drop the bambino, if it's too tight they will start squirming or hollering. Where possible, be the first to reach out, make eye contact, and smile, as the combination of these communicates confidence.

MIRROR THEIR ACTIONS

Mirroring refers to subconsciously imitating the gestures, speech patterns, or attitudes of another person.[18] Couples are notorious for mirroring. Haven't you ever wondered why some partners appear to look and sound alike after years of being together? We tend to mirror people we admire. Which kind of makes me wonder why some people look like their dogs. Who's mirroring who? But I digress. The point is, mirroring doesn't need to be an unconscious action.

Mirroring someone's body language sends subliminal messages of like-mindedness which subsequently builds trust. Whether it's crossing your legs, placing one finger on your cheek,

---

[18] Amy Blaschka (2019) *Science Says To Do This One Thing To Produce The Biggest Results*: Forbes

mirroring says *"Look at me, I'm just like you!"*. Do you think a person who speaks slowly and in a monotone voice would readily build a connection with a high pitched motor mouth going a mile a minute? Not likely.

ASK QUESTIONS ABOUT THEIR FAVOURITE TOPIC...THEMSELVES

Studies show that people spend 60% of conversations talking about themselves.[19] Talking about ourselves triggers our brain's reward system — we get the same good feelings when we have delicious food and when we make the bow-chika-wow-wow (...sex, I'm talking about sex).

Deep down, we're basically narcissistic. Getting people to like you requires catering to that bit of self-centeredness that lies within the other person. You don't want to be too invasive and turn them off. Asking someone pseudo personal questions and expanding on the information they provide always works: *"How was your day? Oh*

---

[19] Adrian Ward (2013) *The Neuroscience of Everybody's Favorite Topic*: Scientific America

really, how's that working out? What do you like about...?" and so on.

If you're looking for a fast way to get someone to open up, ask them about challenges.

Everyone has challenges, and most people find it cathartic to talk about them. This is great if you're on a job interview because it shows what a potential employer sees as a priority. You can then use this knowledge to communicate how you're the solution to those problems. As for more informal conversations, you can use this strategy to build a personal connection. You can frame questions based on the information they've given you: *"Oh, you're a mom? What challenges do you have raising kids and juggling your business?"* But if you don't have anything to go on, ask general questions like these early in the conversation: *"What challenges have you had at work this week?"* or *"What challenges do you have working in your industry?"*

If you want to really rev up your likeability, ask them for advice. It's a huge ego boost because you're telling them that you value their opinion. While this can work with little things like asking which cocktail is the best option at the bar, asking advice about something they value, like their expertise, will be a home run.

BE AN ACTIVE LISTENER

People sometimes mistake being an active listener with having nothing to say. Not true. When you're listening to someone, you're giving thoughtful attention to what they're communicating. Most people tend to hear what someone is talking about, find an area they want to address, and wait their turn to inject a point of view. According to Robin Dreeke, former head of the FBI's Behavioral Analysis Program, you should be asking yourself this question instead: *What idea or thought they mentioned do I find fascinating and want to explore?*[20]

Once you've determined what that is, relay the question and repeat what was said. The fact that you're asking more about the subject and repeating their words verbatim shows the other person that you were listening and care about what they're saying: *"I find that fascinating, can*

---

[20] Melanie Curtin (2020) *7 Ways to Get Someone to Like You, According to an FBI Expert*: INC

you tell me more about why moving to India restored your faith in humanity?"

BE POSITIVELY PLEASANT

By establishing an aura of positivity, the object of your connection will always go back to that image in their mind. You want them to leave the conversation a bit lighter after speaking with you.

Keep these in mind when sharing your fabulous self:

Always greet the object of your connection with a smile. We tend to like people who are happy to see us. Plus, smiling communicates joy, and everyone wants to be around a happy person.

Speak positively. Even if the other person shares some less than sunshine information or seems to be a downer themselves, show empathy, communicate your understanding and offer (if possible or appropriate) a positive perspective. Remember, share your positive perspective and not a solution. It's not your job to fix them.

Compliment other people. *Spontaneous trait transference* is a phenomenon that occurs when people are perceived as possessing the very traits they describe in others.[21] So complimenting other people is another way to have the person you're engaging with to see you in a good light. If you want the other person to think of you as the genuine and intellectual person that you are, find a way to praise someone else with those same qualities.

Show your sense of humour. Laughter is a social glue. When people laugh together, it communicates to both parties that they have similar world views. Don't feel pressured to share prepackaged knock-knock jokes. Plus, if your punchline falls flat you end up looking silly. Here's what you do instead, inject personal stories from your everyday life that have humorous elements. If sitcoms like *Seinfeld* can find the humour in otherwise mundane situations, so can you.

SAY THEIR NAME (A COUPLE TIMES)

Dale Carnegie is widely quoted for saying that a person's name is the sweetest sound in any

---

[21] Skowronski J., Carlston D., Mae L., & Crawford M. (1998) *Spontaneous trait transference: communicators taken on the qualities they describe in others*: National Center for Biotechnology Information, U.S. National Library of Medicine

language for them[22]. This is true. If you don't believe it, have someone call you Kerry in a conversation when your name is Kelly.

You should always make it a point of duty to remember names. Have you ever been in a situation where someone you don't remember greets you by name? You may feel bad temporarily because you forgot who they were, but then you'll feel great knowing that you're significant enough to be remembered. Here are some memory hacks you can use during and after your conversation:

Link the person's name to something you already know. If you met someone named Jane, you could link it to the television show *Jane The Virgin*, the band Maroon 5's first album called *Songs about Jane*, or you're favourite writer *Jane Austen*. Whatever.

Say the other person's name two to three times in the conversation. This is good for fostering a bond as well as storing it in your memory. Once you've heard it, say it at the start of the conversation, during the conversation when

---

[22] Joyce E. A. Russell (2014) *Career Coach: The power of using a name*: Washington Post

you're asking questions, and at the end when you're saying your goodbyes.

Associate their name with weird imagery. It doesn't have to have anything to do with how the person looks, but it helps. If Danielle has a long ponytail, wouldn't it be weird to imagine a cartoon gingerbread man trying to ride her shoulders like a pony and using her hair as reins? Once you've set up that image in your mind, you can repeat to yourself that Danielle is the one with the gingerbread man riding her ponytail.

Type the person's name in your phone right after meeting them. When you get home, write it down in a journal, make a note about what you liked about them along with any other standout qualities. Doing this helps it stay in your long-term memory.

EXUDE CONFIDENCE, BUT SHOW SOME VULNERABILITY

It seems somewhat like an oxymoron, but there's a fine line between appearing overconfident and looking like a wimp. It is what it is, I don't make the rules. Always try to maintain an air of confidence but be willing to share instances where you felt less than 100. It shows that you're self-aware and not too proud to expose what you consider to be weaknesses.

We all have something we're a little insecure about. I remember being in a job interview and they asked how I was feeling. I said "I'm well, thank you. Happy to be here, but I admit I'm a bit nervous!" Everyone can identify with being a little shaky for an interview. Selectively sharing an intimate detail works in your favour because everyone wants to engage with authentic people. When someone shows their vulnerability, it helps to lower the guard of the other person because they can relate to your sincerity (p.s. I got the job).

MAKE EYE CONTACT

Making eye contact makes people feel like you're tuned into what they're saying. It's also a sign of respect and shows your confidence. Since eyes are the window to the soul, by making eye contact you can also safely judge whether or not the other person is receptive to what you're saying.

Too much eye contact can appear rude or awkward. A good rule of thumb is that when you reach a momentary silence in the conversation, you can break your gaze and look off into the horizon for a couple seconds. Be sure not to break your gaze to look at other people. You don't want the person you're engaging with to feel as if they're boring you so you're looking at someone else as an SOS signal for escape.

There's also the inverted triangle method[23] where you draw an imaginary inverted triangle on the other person's face around their eyes and mouth. During the conversation, you can change the gaze every five to ten seconds to each point of the triangle.

DON'T JUDGE THE OBJECT OF YOUR CONNECTION

Judging is an innate defense mechanism. We do it because we want to make sure that who we're engaging with won't harm us. This comes in handy when someone you just met offers you a ride home, but on the flip side, we can go overboard sometimes.

It's easy to misinterpret information and paint someone as evil if you get a hint that their beliefs

---

[23] Lily Zhang (2019) *The Secrets to Making Non-Awkward Eye Contact*: The Muse

contradict your own. Which is why connecting with someone and getting them to like you requires *empathy*. Empathy doesn't mean that you necessarily agree with someone's perspective. It simply means that you're putting yourself in the other person's shoes and increasing your capacity of understanding for who they are.

Let's say that the person you're talking to shares something that kind of rubs you the wrong way. Before you make a snap judgement, really listen to what they're saying and refrain from sharing all the reasons why you don't agree with them. Instead say, *"I never saw it from that perspective, I would love to know why you see it that way."*

Being authentic doesn't mean shoving your opinions down other people's throats.

If being empathetic proves difficult, find one thing you like about the person and focus on that. It could even be their hairstyle. Hold those positive feelings in your mind throughout the conversation. It's all about meeting the other person on their level without compromising who you are.

Keep in mind that it's not just what you say, but what your body language communicates. Be cognizant that raising an eyebrow or folding your arms to an alarming piece of information and acting like you're not phased is noticeable.

There is a phenomenon called *self-verification,* which says that people want to be seen in a way that aligns with the beliefs they have of themselves.[24] It doesn't matter if those views are positive or negative, as long as you believe that the other person sees you how you see yourself. Everyone is the hero in their own story — see them that way. We're all trying to do the best we can with what we have. When you remember that, being non-judgmental comes easy.

EXPECT TO BE LOVED

Go into every opportunity armed with the mindset that everyone will love you. When you do this you increase your likability because you tend to be more open and friendly toward the other person — they call it the *acceptance prophecy.*[25]

---

[24] Shana Lebowitz & Ivan De Luce (2019) *17 psychological tricks to make people like you immediately:* Business Insider
[25] Jeremy Dean (2009) *The Acceptance Prophecy: How You Control Who Likes Yo*

Listen, you know you're awesome. Even though the skills you've learned is about how to build rapport with other people, don't forget that you're an important part of the equation. So, relax. Every conversation is an opportunity to share who you are.

Be open to learning about the other person, but contribute your stories too. Since you know that people tend to like people who are like them, you can kick things off by emphasizing shared values. Listen keenly to things you have in common. You may realize that they value *adventure* because their stories include skydiving and backpacking through Europe. Even if you've never done either of those things, if you value adventure too, you can share your excitement for what they've done along with similar experiences you've had.

CHAPTER FOURTEEN

HOW TO BUILD RELATIONSHIPS ONLINE

Networking isn't confined to live events. Some of my most valuable connections have been made online. It takes the pressure off. You can spend time cultivating relationships there until they turn into face-to-face conversations. Since you've set the foundation beforehand, any nervousness you would have had about meeting someone new will be pretty much non-existent.

MAKE MEANINGFUL CONTRIBUTIONS TO PRIVATE GROUPS

There are literally millions of groups online. So it makes sense to join a few related to your industry and personal interests. Since private groups are exclusive in nature, members see it as a safe space to ask questions and connect with people like them. Groups tend to have a high level of engagement, so it's important that you participate in conversations often to stand out. Plus, it gives you the opportunity to share your knowledge and magnetic personality. Consistently offering value will attract the attention of other members' who need your expertise, which opens the door for collaboration.

Don't go overboard with joining multiple groups. Select about 3 -5 that you can really sink your teeth into. You want to be able to invest enough of your time to make contributions on a regular basis.

SHOW THAT YOU'RE INVESTED FOR THE LONG HAUL

Take the time to comment on other people's social media posts. We're not talking about low value comments like the high-five emoji. Leave a thoughtful message. Commenting gives you an edge. Check it out for yourself. Influencers can get thousands of likes for something but only a few comments by comparison. When someone sees that you have a genuine interest in them and their passions, they'll take notice. Now if you happen to share their post with a thoughtful comment *and* mention them in updates, you're likely going to get an immediate response. It pays to be consistent.

Sometimes you have to engage with the object of your connection's content over a couple of months before they take notice. If that seems too long, then you're not serious enough about getting to know them.

SHOUT OUT OTHER BUSINESSES

Is there a product or service you absolutely love? Or maybe someone in your industry copped an award. I'm a firm believer in *collaboration over competition*. If you feel positive vibes about a fellow business owner or their product, take the time to promote it on your blog and social media platforms. Not only are you doing your part to empower other entrepreneurs, you attract attention and increase your chances of getting referrals from the object of your connection.

SEND A DIRECT MESSAGE ON SOCIAL MEDIA

Once you've built up a reputation of being an attentive and loyal follower, introduce yourself by sending a direct message. You can drop a line simply to say hello and let them know how much you admire what they do and their content.

If you want to dive in and try to make a partnership, let your message be brief, and ask if you can share further details with them via email. This has worked for me immensely because:

A. you take out the SPAM factor by sharing specifically what you admire about them

B. you get right to the point of sharing your mission and making the request

C. you give the other person the opportunity to accept or reject your request to share further information.

That last part is important because no one is obligated to support you. If you give them an option, you're likely to get a favourable response. One more thing, don't be disheartened if you don't get an answer right away or even at all. You can try again at a later date while moving onto another prospect. I like to reach out at least two times spaced out within a week or two. Keep in mind that the object of your connection may have missed the message or forgot to respond.

If you want help, be straight up and ask for it.

I operate under the principle that if something positive about someone comes to mind, you shouldn't hesitate to tell them. I do it with friends, family, colleagues, even people I've never met. One time I reached out to a fabulous influencer who I thought did a phenomenal job of sharing her faith through her business' brand without alienating people with other beliefs. Because of her level of success I really didn't expect a response, I just wanted to share some love. But guess what, she did respond. The lady with hundreds of thousands of followers took the time to answer moi. She said that comment really made her day because it was always something at the forefront of her mind. My simple private message made an impact and we've had a solid relationship ever since.

SUBSCRIBE TO THEIR NEWSLETTER

A newsletter is like an exclusive club. If someone gives you their email address, they're saying that they value what you have to say and want to be part of your inner circle. So, it's a highly personal means of communication for the owner.

Someone I had supported in a business relationship unsubscribed from my mailing list once the deal was over. I was surprised, and I felt used. She seemed to be really into having a genuine friendship. Clearly they only wanted to connect because knowing me served their self-serving purpose. Several months down the road, they reached out and claimed that they were not getting my newsletters the day after myself and some other women I supported were featured in a popular magazine. Coincidence? I think not. People do make mistakes. Either way, I'm more cautious when dealing with that person. Something to think about.

GIVE THEM SHARE-WORTHY CONTENT

People remember when you've assisted them with something they actually needed. Ask yourself what benefit the other person gets out of having a relationship with you, and see how you can offer that.

Another option is to give them something they can use. Scan the person's brand, and create image quotes using their own words. Not only have you stroked their ego, but you've also saved them the time it would take to create content for themselves. You don't have to be a graphic artist to do this, *Canva* is a great option for creating quick and attractive designs. But if you are a creative soul, this allows you to show off your skills.

CHAPTER FIFTEEN

REMOVE ROTTEN NARRATIVES

Buddist monks don't achieve enlightenment during their first meditation. I guess they could, but I never heard of one. Can you imagine the book sales for *Learn how to get to nirvana in 24 hours*? Instant bestseller.

Stories can be a catalyst for growth and reinvention. The reverse is also true. Our interpretation of experiences can keep us trapped in a loop of negativity and despair. The wonderful thing about being a human on this green and blue cosmic marble is that we have consciousness. It's that gift of self-awareness and the power of choice is what makes us creative forces of nature. So like monks on a mission to achieve nirvana, you have to be intentional about your success. This requires a higher frequency of thinking, which can be cultivated through the consistent and honest appraisal of your inner stories.

Storytelling is a valuable skill for influencing others, but it goes both ways. If you feel stuck in any area of your life, it's time to change the story.

This requires being honest with yourself about your experiences and rejiggering toxic ways of thinking about ourselves, other people, and the world.

You can reframe your reality by shifting your internal narrative.

No matter where I go, people see me as an energizer bunny. Seriously, for anonymous appraisals multiple people wrote "energized bunny". Though hearing this always warms my heart, for many years I was a hot mess on the inside. I was the voice for the voiceless and a wellspring of positivity for those who needed it. But I couldn't keep it together for myself. When I got home everything fell apart. I would complain bitterly about work, from my salary to two-faced bosses.

When I reached the limit of crap I could take, I split. Maybe it's the millennial in me. But still, nothing changed. I kept meeting the same kinds of people and getting paid peanuts. I was stuck in dead-end jobs for years until my husband pointed out that I was the common denominator. How. Dare. He. But on second thought, was it really me all along? It had to be. Changing the environment didn't work, it even seemed to get worse.

When your boss tells you that giving orphaned interns a stipend is wrong because "giving them handouts doesn't teach them about the world" things are pretty bad. But no matter how toxic a situation is, you shouldn't let it change you into something ugly. So I made the decision to change my internal narrative from "I don't deserve to be here" to "I'm here for a higher purpose". Maybe I was placed in those situations not for myself, but for others. Maybe coworkers needed my light and energy, and maybe I needed those crazy experiences to build my muscle for future experiences.

I kid you not, reinterpreting my situation changed everything. Now when colleagues and clients need some support on how to navigate crazy situations in their career my heart smiles, because I have the tools to help them.

Life is subjective. The same event can happen to different people and interpret it differently. There is no right or wrong way to interpret the adventures and setbacks we've had, but we can choose to be an impartial critic or get carried away with our emotions.

REPRESENT YOURSELF AS IF YOU WERE A CLIENT

Even the most confident woman can forget who she is for a moment when faced with something new and scary.

A few years ago, I directed a video featuring a few entrepreneurs on the rise. Now, not everyone is cool being in front of a camera. Totally understandable. But I noticed that when the men forgot a line, they paused and started again. When the women forgot, they kept apologizing. They were beating themselves up over nothing. As a woman this drove me crazy, but I kept reassuring the ladies that it was fine and that they really shouldn't consider it a mistake. Just stop and start again.

I woke up at 5:35 a.m. because I was super excited to print my business cards. For me, it represented an evolution in my career. Customer service is a big deal for me. Probably because I had to deal with crazy passengers when I worked in the airline industry (if I can keep my cool with a screaming nutjob who acts as if it's my fault they left their passport on the plane, anyone can do it). So when I arrived at the printers later that morning, getting assisted by a pleasant college student promised that the rest of the day would be great.

After a long wait, I got the cards back and discovered that they weren't cut right. Anyone who knows me knows how precise I am with everything. I even put cut lines on the graphic so that this exact scenario wouldn't happen. Needless to say, I was disappointed. The day started off so well. I wanted it to be reprinted, but I kept thinking about the nice girl. How could I get mad at her?

If I was representing a client that thought wouldn't have entered my head. I would have nicely but firmly asked her to do it over. Firmly, because she had to know that what she was giving me wasn't good. Instead, I held back.

Stop apologizing for nothing.

It's easier to be a ball-buster if the person on the receiving end is a douche. But because I valued her pleasant nature, thoughts about hurting her feelings entered my mind – maybe I was making too big a deal about it.

So, I left the store with uneven cards. I told my husband what went down. Some of his cards weren't cut right either. This made me even more upset, but I was still reluctant to make a move. Kevin could see how much it bothered me. He kept assuring me that it was acceptable to ask them to do it over, and I kept lying to him and myself saying that it was fine. After about three minutes of this, he let me know that we weren't leaving the parking lot until I went back and got it fixed. So annoying.

I headed straight to the young woman and requested that the cards be done over. This small yet empowering action filled me with great satisfaction, and only a tinge of guilt. And you know what? She didn't hate me. She did her job with a smile.

Kevin was to me like I was to those women entrepreneurs. Even though the words didn't escape my lips, there I was apologizing for nothing. I was willing to take the road of least resistance for fear of appearing mean to the nice lady.

There won't always be someone to remind you of your power and make you do the uncomfortable things. But I want you to come to terms with the fact that once you decide to raise your standards, you have to keep them there. When it comes to owning your worth, no action is ever little. You deserve the best life has to offer. You deserve to stop and start again.

YOUR SUBCONSCIOUS IS LISTENING

If you accept substandard work then that's what you're gonna get. Remember, your subconscious is always listening. You have to take notice if you're constantly making excuses about not getting what you know deep down you deserve. It can be as simple as not letting the seamstress know that you think that the shoulder pads in the suit she made you is a little too 1980s because you're afraid to hurt her feelings. Besides, she's nice and she's pushing 60. Now there you are walking into business meetings looking like an extra from the movie *Working Girls*.

It really isn't about the clothes. If you have a powerhouse presence, what you're wearing makes little difference. But in your mind, your confidence is shaken and your subconscious says *"Well, she's wearing it. This must be what she deserves"*. Eventually, you'll have a closet full of clothes that, taking a page out of Marie Kondo's playbook, doesn't bring you joy.

Never settling for less than excellence goes beyond the material stuff. It's about how our actions (and inaction) affect the stories we tell ourselves and how that has a significant impact on how we operate in the world.

You don't attract what you want, you attract what you tolerate.

Cara ran a coaching programme and noticed that clients kept missing their 1:1 sessions. She got fed up one day and fired them. Yeah, she gave them a refund and told them see ya later. What she realized was that she kept attracting what she tolerated — lazy clients. She was invested in their growth more than they were and was tired of making excuses for them. Within a few months, she started getting serious clients because she was clear in her messaging about who she was and what she expected from people who work with her. Once you raise your standards, it's difficult to go back to who you once were.

BE COMMITTED TO YOURSELF

A promise is a comfort to a fool. That's what I heard when my 5 year old self made the mistake of leaving a half-eaten bag of Skittles in the fridge. I intended to eat it later in the afternoon while I chilled with my juice box watching Super Grover. But alas, my father had other plans. I made him promise not to eat it and he agreed. A few hours later, I'd see him walking down the hall chugging down my candy. Wanting to cry, scream, and kick him in the shins all at the same time, all I could manage to get out was a simple question: Why?

Finding this deliciously hilarious, my father smirked and said that a promise was a comfort to a fool.

Did that I mean I was a fool?
What was a fool anyway?
I'm sure it can't be good.
But, why did he promise in the first place?

Unless you've been living in a bubble on the moon, you know very well that life doesn't move in a straight line. Whether it's for a legitimately good reason like to protect someone from harm, or because you're a pre-diabetic man with a sugar craving the size of Texas, pinkie-swears are sometimes broken.

But it makes you wonder about the whole promise thing. Why should I, you, anyone, accept or keep them? A promise is an investment of trust and commitment. We often think about promises in the context of our relationship with another person. I want you to think about the promises you make to yourself. Whether you realize it or not, every decision you make is a promise to your future. Dreaming about running a million dollar multi-media empire but using your spare time to gossip with your mother about how 65 year old Auntie Sally dresses too sexy for her age doesn't help you achieve your goal. Those are unconscious promises. The fruits of those promises sneak up on you years down the road when Auntie Sally still dresses the way she does and you're still stuck in a dead-end job.

Now let's talk about conscious promises. When you break promises to yourself, you're basically telling your subconscious that you can't be trusted. If you doubt me, think about it. When someone breaks a promise, especially if it's consistent, your trust in them chips away bit by bit. You see them as unreliable, unworthy of your trust. Break promises to yourself consistently, and you'll have the same perspective.

This is why it's especially hard to stay on diets (and here you thought it was because cauliflower smells like dank socks). You start out energized, do great for a day or two, then beat yourself up when you realize that you've eaten six frosted cupcakes within 15 minutes after a midnight craving went haywire.

Promising yourself to success means not taking no for an answer, and letting your mission be bigger than your ego or your fear. People always ask me how I get so many amazing high-profile women on my show *The Digital Boss Babe Podcast* and the answer always shocks them – I ask them. I slide into their DMs and I simply ask. Sure, sometimes I get nervous before asking, but then I put on my big girl skirt and just go for it. The worst that can happen is that I get a no or no answer at all. That's not enough to stop me pushing onward, especially since my promise to educate is not for me, it's for ambitious ladies. It's for you.

DON'T WAIT TO BE GIVEN WHAT YOU WANT

I always hated waiting. Growing up I always got what I needed but hardly ever what I wanted. I mean, if you ask for a guitar as a graduation present and give up going to prom so there'd be enough money to get one, you don't expect a mini-stereo. Right, mother? I can laugh about it now. I mean she was a single mom surviving on a secretary's salary. I couldn't appreciate the effort and thoughtfulness behind the gift. No guitar, but here's music. Anyway, I digress. The point is, I was pissed.

So what did I do? I worked hard and saved my money till I got it, beautiful blue Palmers guitar. Do I play? If *Twinkle Twinkle Little Star* counts then yes. But it hangs on my wall to this day as a reminder of a time when I finally got fed up with waiting.

Sure, there's something to be said for patience. Patience is what you use when you see a clear outcome. When your gut tells you that standing still is the best option. Once the owner of a company hung a management position over my head for a year. He said I was too ambitious and that I should continue doing a great job and wait. Too ambitious? As crazy as that sounded, I waited.

Deep down, I was skeptical that my goal would see fruition because his actions with other people gave me hints that *maybe* I shouldn't hold my breath. One year later, I was introduced to the new marketing manager. Ouch, that hurt. But I was mostly upset that I was so foolish to wait. When I asked about it, I was told that they were temporary and that I should still hold on. By then,

I knew my value and trusted my intuition when it said to move on.

I got a new job within a month and instantly fell in love with my supervisor. She was a mentor without even knowing it. She empowered me in so many ways and let me know from the beginning that she wanted to have me promoted. I was still gun shy from my last experience, but something told me this was the real deal. So I decided to remove the rotten narrative that people in power can't be trusted. A little over a year later, I was promoted to a bigger position than what I once coveted from my other job.

ALL THAT GLITTERS ISN'T FRIENDSHIP

On your rise to the top people will want to hang on your coattails. For a really long time I would admire women who seemed to have every aspect of their life together. I would see them on television and all over social media promoting their business and hanging with the same groups of people.

I was never one of those cool kids growing up. You know the ones I'm talking about, the pretty ones all the boys loved and skipped class to drink beer.

I never understood why that was considered the thing to do, but there you go.

They kept me out of their cliques because I was the girl who hung out with the nerds, dorks and dweebs. Which never bothered me really, I wanted real connection and that's what I got from my cartoon watching peeps. But as a teenager, exclusion sometimes makes you wonder if something's wrong with you. Fast forward into adulthood, I got better at socializing with all kinds of people. Soon I was invited to the inner circle of women I always admired. They had shiny things, perfect hair and clothes, and could network like nobody's business.

Eventually I realized that most of these women didn't actually like each other. They banded together for image purposes only and stepped on whoever they needed to get where they wanted to go. It was then that I realized that staying in my own lane and carving out my own path was a blessing. The inner narrative from high school wondering if I was weird for not fitting in with all types of people, transformed into "God was protecting me from those kinds of people".

Do you remember the story of *Julius Caesar*? It's a story about ambition that ends with his assassination — a conspiracy orchestrated by someone he considered to be his friend. *Et tu, Brutus?*

Jealousy is a funny thing. It creeps in when you least expect it. With all of the good inside of you, be aware that we don't live in a perfect world. As it was for me, and many others before, the same people who excluded you will eventually be the ones begging to be part of your winning team. Don't be fooled by the bright lights and smiles. Stay firmly planted in your values and always do an appraisal of who should be in your space.

MMM...CALLALOO QUICHE

What comes to mind when you think about *networking*? If you're like most people, after you've gotten over the initial dread that accompanies the thought of putting yourself out there, you probably think it's simply a means to an end to get contacts. A necessary evil that only extroverts and people scheming their way up the corporate ladder do best.

You may even feel that the whole activity isn't for you. After all, why should you have to build relationships simply to get ahead in life? I totally agree. You shouldn't have to. The entire premise is icky. But here's the thing, you're thinking about it all *wrong*.

I used to be one of those people who had the wrong mindset. Not only did networking feel like a colossal waste of my time, I hated the idea that I had to basically sell myself to someone whom I may or may not really like at the end of the day. Also, there was no guarantee that the person I was trying to bond with would remember me past that initial meeting, or be so benevolent to make my professional dreams a reality. It seemed manipulative and felt super exhausting. Needless to say, I was never good at it. Being inauthentic was not my bag, baby.

After years of resigning myself to chow down on free food at corporate events, something changed one day. I got *really* bored. So much so that I had to speak to someone. Anyone. I started opening up to other attendees at my table by commenting on the quiche and how attractive the room was. I eventually started to walk around and introduce myself to people just to start a conversation. I was interested in what they thought of that delicious quiche and what they were doing there. I wanted to get to know them. No agenda. No selling.

By the time our meeting of the minds was over I realized that people started asking for my business card ...even if we never got around to talking about business. That's when it clicked: *networking didn't have to be a vapid exchange.* It could be about building a meaningful connection with another person. Go figure.

I was in the driver's seat. I gave cards to who I liked and wanted to get to know better both personally and professionally. This little mental shift made networking a whole lot easier because it felt right in my soul. I was getting to know the person beyond the business and they were getting to know me in a real way.

People can tell if someone's chatting them up to use them for something. If you don't like it, why should they? Your mission when networking should always be to see how you can support the person you're connecting with. Actively listen to them and see how you can support them in non-monetary ways. This means to avoid trying to sell them on your business products or services. Instead, offer to meet after the event and share advice. You can even open the opportunity to connect them to other people in your network. I've done this countless times. Not only does helping people make your relationships richer, it makes you feel good.

Success happens when opportunity meets preparation. Before going to networking events, get as much information as you can on the speakers, topics, and other individuals who might be in attendance. Store everything in your phone if you need a refresher. This way, you can wow people with your seemingly natural ability to be in the know. Store a few conversation starters too and glance at them whenever you're gearing up to talk to someone. Here are some you can use after you've passed the introduction phase:

What was the last funny video you saw?

What do you do to get rid of stress?

What did you do last weekend?

What three words best describe you?

What's your favorite way to waste time?

Do you have any pets? What are their names?

What did you do on your last vacation?

Who in your life brings you the most joy?

What is the most annoying habit you think someone can have?

Where is the most beautiful place you've been?

Who was your best friend in elementary school?

We go to networking events to meet people. Remember that someone, or even a couple someones, are there to meet you. They want to connect with you on a personal level, and they need your specific skills to help them grow.

RE-WRITE YOUR STORIES

As you can see, what we tell ourselves can easily become obstacles to our success, both personally and professionally.

We can easily create stories from our past that limit our potential by focusing on the pain instead of the results. So instead of repeating the narrative "my father didn't show me love and wasn't a good provider" one could focus on the results, which could be "my father did the best with the tools he was given, thanks to this experience I know what qualities I want in a partner".

It's critical to review the stories you're telling yourself. If it makes you feel bad or anxious, reinterpret the lesson. Check in with yourself everyday and ask yourself these questions:

1. What were the rotten/negative narratives created from this experience?

2. How has thinking this way limited me?

3. What good has come from the experience?

If you're having trouble seeing the positives, confide in someone you trust or a trained professional (that's what they're there for) who can help you see the situation from another perspective. Once you've identified the "objective good", you can arm yourself with new stories that support your continuous growth and transformation.

FINAL THOUGHTS

TAKE A CHANCE ON LASAGNA

I want to close with one more food story.

When I was around 8 years old, my Grandma Mary plopped a plate of lasagna in front of me. "Eat" she said. It looked weird. I had never seen anything like it. It was orangy-red and looked like a glob of mush. With my face covered in grimace I gave a firm "No", something I had never said to her before. She sweetly responded, "Eat. You'll like it". Steadfast in my objection, I gave a much more polite "No, thank you".

Then the Irish rage I knew all too well bubbled over as she shouted "EAT!". I had no choice. I started to slowly navigate the lasagna and took my first death-defying bite and...it was freaking' amazing!

With her fire instantaneously cooled, she gave a beaming smile "See? I told you you'd like it".

Lasagna is one of my all-time fave dishes. What would have happened if I never tasted it? Is there even life without lasagna?! Looking back, I can see now that that was the moment I became obsessed with Italian food. If I couldn't get the real deal, I would imagine that Ramen noodles was freshly made spaghetti and that ketchup was bolognese sauce. Who knows, if my grandmother didn't scare me into submission I probably wouldn't have ended up vacationing in Rome with my love muffin years later.

Can you see how easy it can be to miss out on something that has the potential to change our lives? It's the same way when we really want to make a transformation but something holds us back — hard work, people's perceptions, it could be anything. For my younger self, it was a fear of the unknown. Fear is healthy. It can protect us. But since you're long past those tender years, you're better able to make the distinction on how fear may be limiting your potential.

Unlike my grandma, no one is going to force you to do what's necessary to grow your brand or design the life and business of your dreams. But I want you to think about your lasagna, and what you'd be missing out on if you don't dig in. Don't wait another minute.

ABOUT THE AUTHOR

Gizelle Riley teaches new and emerging leaders from startups to Fortune 500 companies how to build magnetic digital brands and become charismatic communicators.

With over a decade working in media and communications, her expertise in interpersonal intelligence, storytelling, and public relations has supported the expert positioning of countless professionals.

A self-professed "outgoing introvert", Gizelle's work has been featured in major publications around the world, including *Huffington Post*, *Virgin*, *Thrive Global*, *Wonder Forest*, and *Caribbean Posh*.

She lives in Kingston, Jamaica with her husband Kevin and sugar dumplin' son Gabe. Get to know her better at **www.gizelleriley.com**

ACKNOWLEDGEMENTS

I'm so grateful for every experience God has given me on this crazy ride of life. Some were unpleasant, most were exciting, but each one was a lesson. Without them, I wouldn't have been able to write this book and step into my boss babe-ness.

Gabriel, having you makes me strive to be the best version of myself every day. Kevin, my husband and best friend, thank you for being my loving ass-kicker.

To my mom Cheryl, the water to my earth, thank you for planting dreams and giving me everything you had so that I could thrive. Thank you Gama 'Lainie and Grandma Mary, my first examples of badass women.

Thank you Grandpa 'Lonzo, whose soul-awakening books I would steal, and to my dad Jeffrey who kickstarted my passion for stories by teaching (and forcing) me to read.

Made in the USA
Columbia, SC
24 November 2020